HIRING YOUR GHOST

Essential Guide to Find and Hire the Perfect Ghostwriter and Launch Your Book

Written by

Jeffrey A. Mangus

Copyright

Ghostwriting USA/JAM Books 2020© All rights reserved. No part of this publication may be reproduced, stored in a retrieval system, or transmitted in any form or by any means—for example, electronic, photocopy, recording—without the written permission of the publisher and author. The only exceptions are brief quotations in printed reviews.

Published by Jeffrey Allen Mangus/ Ghostwriting USA-JAM Books 2020©
Printed in The United States of America
Editor: Anne Weise

Some names and details may have been changed to protect the privacy of individuals.

ISBN-979-86-3590-462-6
ISBN-978-01-0878-846-5
Library of Congress Control Number-

Author-Jeffrey A. Mangus CEO-Ghostwriting USA
Http://www.ghostwritingusa.com

Contents

PROLOGUE 3

Phase One "WHAT" 7

Introduction 9

Chapter 1/ What is the Ghostwriter's Role and Engagement? 13

Chapter 2/ WHAT Publishing Plan to Take with Your Ghostwriter . 21

Phase TWO "WHO" 33

Chapter 3/ WHO Needs to Find and Hire a Ghostwriter? 35

Phase 3 "WHY" 41

Chapter 4/ Deciding "WHY" to Hire a Ghostwriter 43

Phase 4 "WHEN" 61

Chapter 5/ Knowing "When" to Hire a Ghostwriter 63

Phase 5 "Where" 73

Chapter 6/ Knowing "Where" to Find and Hire the "Write" Ghostwriter 75

Phase 6 "How" 81

Chapter 7/ How to See the Red Flags in Ghost Hunting 83

Chapter 8/ How Ghostwriter Fees are Explained 106

Chapter 9/How to Choose the Best Ghostwriter 122

Chapter 10/ Ghostwriting Contracts Explained 133

Chapter 11/How to Hire, Work with and Know the Process with Your New Ghostwriter 150

Chapter 12/ How to Plan Your Book 161

Chapter 13/ How a Ghostwriter and Author Collaboration Works 167

Chapter 14/ How to Execute Your Book with Your Ghostwriter 174

Chapter 15/ A Book Is Born 191

Chapter 16/ Ghostwriter Hunt Finale 205

About the Author **209**

Sources **211**

Acknowledgments

Thank you to all of my clients past, present, and future. Without you my ghostwriting life would not be possible.

Thank you to my wife Kelly for always being there, loving me through for better or for worse.

Thank you to all of my kids, Brady, Ryann, Gabby, Jacob, and Sophie. Thanks for believing.

Thank you to Warren Tuttle, Gary Krebs, Derek Lewis for helping me get to where I am today with my ghostwriting.

2

PROLOGUE

Hello, fellow writers and authors. Thank you for picking up this book. You are here I will assume for one specific thing— to find the best way to hire the perfect ghostwriter for your book. This book is for everyone who has a book writing plan or dream. Whether you are an expert in your field of business, a Fortune 500 leader, CEO, celebrity, musician, artist, or individual with a story to tell—I wrote this book for you.

Over the years, I have discovered many people need help with the book-writing process and the understanding of collaboration between a ghostwriter and author. The first issue most misunderstood is hiring a ghostwriter to pen your book is seen as an unethical practice. It is not. The problem is in today's society is there are too many variables, options, blogs, videos, choices, opinions, and fears about ghostwriters and ghostwriting services. All these factors add up, and after a while, create massive confusion and chaos about choosing the right ghostwriter for your book.

I wanted to write a book that would set the record straight finally and for once end the confusion. My intention is to help new authors find ghostwriters that fit their budget and personality. I want this book to be your go-to guide in understanding ghostwriters, their process, their value, and how to write a book utilizing the services of a ghostwriter. Yet, the question that materialized most in my brain was, how *could I do it— and most of all, do it right?*

So, I sat down and considered the best route to take in writing this book because I knew the approach had to be true—and right. Then it hit me. I remembered in school (junior high if I recall) where I was taught about six major questions to ask when facing a significant problem. You can achieve answers to problems by asking the following: *Who, What, Why, When, Where, and How.* I mean, writers and journalists have been using these questions for years to generate articles, news releases, and even press releases—and so could I.

Why wouldn't they work for the book because, throughout my professional ghostwriting days, these thought-provoking questions are a reoccurrence in most of my new client conversations. And most, if not all, are based upon these simplistic inquisitive factors. For example, the

questions I receive, such as:
- **Who** have you written for?
- **What** are your prices?
- **When** can you get started?
- **Why** does it take so long to write a book?
- **Where** can I find out how to self-publish?
- **How** do you capture my voice?

In honor of doing what is best for every author client and any new author out there in the world, I felt compelled to write and answer the basic questions—and then dig deeper. The intent is to make this easy and allow you to glean the information you need to make your book happen.

The book is broken down into sections based upon each factor of *Who, What, Why, When, Where, and How*. The book does NOT have to be read in consecutive order, and you can skip around. Yet, I encourage you to start at the beginning and read it through. It is my hope you walk away with an increased understanding of hiring and working with a ghostwriter and everything that is involved throughout the process.

One last thing—this book is not a gigantic sales pitch for my services, yet, I discuss in immense detail on how I operate my ghostwriting business from the inside out. If you are a new author and do want to talk to me, there is information at the end of the book explaining how to do so. I would love to learn how I can help.

As a ghostwriter, what I enjoy the most is talking to new authors about their new books. I love to learn about people's exciting lives and unique perspectives. For me, I believe my job as a ghostwriter is an honorable and humbling position to have an opportunity to talk to great and ingenious people across the country about their books. This brings me to the heart and soul of this book because it was derived from talking to people who have many questions about the ghostwriting process. Within the following pages and chapter, I will do my best to reveal the inner workings of working with a ghostwriter. I have taken on the task of explaining in-depth detail on how the book writing and publishing process works from an author and ghostwriting viewpoint, plus guide you in launching your new book.

A special note for my fellow ghostwriters everywhere,

My fellow ghostwriters, kudos to you, your skills, talent, and your passion for writing. My hope is this book helps you with your business endeavors by urging new authors to seek you out for their book projects.

Best to you all,
Jeffrey Allen Mangus

Phase One "WHAT"

WHAT is Involved with Finding a Ghostwriter for Your Book?

Introduction

Over the years, as a professional ghostwriter, I have found an overwhelming, ever-present need for new authors to understand ghostwriters. One would think most people understand the concept of ghostwriters, yet, many new authors do not fully understand the reason and process. However, I am not going to pretend to insult your intelligence by discussing basic understanding and concepts of what a ghostwriter is and does. I am going to assume you have grasped the idea, and I don't want to begin by delivering basement level drivel and fill the pages with unnecessary words for the sake of putting words to paper about ghostwriting. My intent is pure, to provide you the exact method to go about hiring the perfect ghostwriter for your book project.

Now, I do know that by writing a book of this nature, there will be new authors who choose other ghostwriters, other than myself, to write their books. My motives are clear and as crazy as this sounds— I hope you do. We all are different and have different tastes, and some of you may like me, and some may not. This is why I wanted the book to be broad and provide choices for you as a new author. I wanted to reveal a broader horizon to allow you to choose the best ghostwriter for you and your project. Because if it were one-sided, pointing just to me and my services, —it would not do you any justice.

I genuinely hope that you find the perfect ghostwriter match for your project. I want you to locate the one person who you deem worthy of helping you see your book come to life and, most of all— for you to enjoy the journey. That is the entire intent of this book, and I believe if more people had better writing experiences with ghostwriters, more projects could get underway, and more books made available for our society. What is wrong with that, right?

Nonetheless, if at any point along the way, you feel that I may be the one who can help you make it happen, then, by all means, let's talk. I would love nothing more than to help you write your book. And I'm aware I am going to lose some clients to other great ghostwriters. I can't be THE go-to ghostwriter to ALL the new authors out there, can I?

My goal is to help you in searching to find the perfect ghostwriter that will help you and your book to be successful. I will not pretend to be shy and say that I would love to learn about you as a new author and any potential ideas you have for a book. But the intention of this book sincere and not sugarcoated, glazed over, with pages filled with irrelevant, on-the-surface information. You are here because you are ready to write a book, and my goal is to go deep into helping you in finding the perfect ghostwriter that fits your style, matches your business book plans, or for yourself.

Writing a book is a dream for most people, and the journey of writing and seeing a book come to life is one that is fulfilling. Companies and businesses have recognized the need for books, and yet the mission of finding the right ghostwriter is filled with obstacles and challenges that most do not want to face.

Perhaps you are here because you, as a new author, recognize the need to hire a ghostwriter as the first step into becoming a published author. Yet, maybe you are a hard-working business person, and you just do not have the time to write a book. Or possibly, you simply understand you do not possess the skills or the drive to learn how to write a book, and this is why you're thinking of hiring a ghostwriter.

Whatever the reason, give yourself accolades because preparing to hire a ghostwriter to get your book or books out into the world is a smart, humbling, professional, and savvy decision. With this book, I will provide the most thorough knowledge and ghostwriting industry information to help you begin your journey in obtaining the services of the perfect ghostwriter to make your dreams come true.

So, I want you to settle in, kick back, and pop open a cold one and get ready to transform your life. This book will guide every step of the way in seeking the ghostwriter that fits you, your life, and budget to make the ambitions of your book a reality.

Chapter 1/ What is the Ghostwriter's Role and Engagement?

"Every individual has a role to play for the betterment of our nation."

~ **Sunday Adelaja,** *The Mountain of Ignorance*

I have over the past six years as a full-time ghostwriter written multiple books to my credit. Yet, it is only until now that I feel competent and equally qualified to talk about what exactly ghostwriters do. I believe, along with understanding essential why you want to write a book, that realizing what ghostwriters do and their specific roles in the book process are vital in your search.

What does a ghostwriter do? This is a broad question. By definition, a ghostwriter is a writer that companies, CEOs, individuals, and new potential new authors hire to write a book for a fee. The catch to ghostwriting is the ghostwriter receives the payment instead of acquiring credit for the writing work produced. Ghostwriters are involved in many different writing projects, such as:

- Book manuscripts

- Speeches
- Scripts
- Screenplays
- Articles
- Webpages
- Blogs
- Short stories
- Songs
- Lyrics
- Social Media Posts

New authors (like you) hire the ghostwriter, and you receive the writing credit. Some people believe this is an unethical practice. For those with doubting minds, ghostwriting is entirely ethical. Why? Simple, even though you didn't physically write the words, the words, stories, events, experiences, and skills are uniquely yours and yours alone.

The ghostwriter is merely a vessel for the work and paid in advance of completing the project through payment arrangements and is considered a "work for hire." And this means the ghostwriter remains in the background and doesn't receive any credit for the work unless specified as "cover credit."

Once again, ghostwriting is neither illegal nor unethical, and in today's busy world, it is accepted as a common practice. In most ghostwriting situations by celebrities, politicians, or business entities, the author does not possess the writing skills or time to produce a professional, saleable manuscript.

So, they employ a professional ghostwriter who does. The ghostwriter is expected to produce high-quality writing that reads smoothly, cohesively, and professionally, plus, capture the essence of the author's specific voice. Simply put—a ghostwriter helps authors (you) write your book by proxy.

Ghostwriters Understand Audience and Voice

One primary question I often receive is how do I capture the author's voice? I admit when I first became a ghostwriter, this task appeared to be confusing as hell. *How can I capture another person's voice?* I asked myself. The answer—difficult work and countless hours behind the keyboard; studying each author's tone, diction, voice, annunciation, and words, and phrases.

It did not come easy, with many trials, errors, and retries to get it right. There was some blood and more than a few tears along the way, yet, I persevered and trudged forward with vigor, eager to hone my craft. Even today, when I begin a new book project, it takes a few chapters to dial in the tone and style of an author. However, I've learned to get the project off on the right foot, I make it known upfront that it will take a chapter or two to make things flow. I explain to the author what to expect, and this reduces miscommunication and helps make the process flow more manageable.

As a ghostwriter, capturing the voice of an author is the number one skill I possess. It is the essential ingredient that I place in high regard as an esteemed value upon every new author I work for. Each author client has their own unique style and inflection, and a good ghostwriter should be able to capture your voice. Remember, no one is going to get your voice precisely like yours. That is impossible, yet, a good ghostwriter should come extremely close to how you phrase sentences, use words, dialects, idioms, and tone. Be patient as it may take a few chapters to home in on your voice and style.

You, as a new author, must learn to compromise and give the ghostwriter some leeway to dial in the words that best represent you. It will take patience, and often, at first, it can be hard to read your story written by someone else. This is always a struggle I experience with my new authors, and again, I do my best to soften the blow and explain how they might encounter those odd feelings.

The goal for me is to write to where the reader would not know that the author did not write the work. That is my job–to be hidden, be the ghostwriter, and make it authentic with the author's words behind the scenes. As a professional ghostwriter, I provide upfront advice on what to expect in these situations. Any ghostwriter you speak to should explain the process in detail.

I help the author through the experience, overcome the challenges, and resolve any confusion. Plus, understanding the writing process helps the author see the work with transparent expectancies and read and review the work openly—without bias.

As you search for the ghostwriter for your project, ask about voice and their skills in capturing an author's voice. Ask how the ghostwriter plans to catch your words. What is their method used to find your voice as the author? Voice and making the reader believe, ultimately, it is you, the author is an essential part of the ghostwriting process. Remember, most of all, your ghostwriter must possess this skill. If not, what is the point?

A professional ghostwriter listens and studies your tone, inflection, and the style of your voice. Listening and learning about you is the first critical step any ghostwriter you are considering should do. I have found the challenge gratifying and fascinating to write in my author's voice and style. The best results are achieved when I immerse myself deeply into the author's life, almost as if I'm living vicariously through someone else. Sort of like acting in a play just for a little while, and I get to pretend to be someone else as I write. It's uplifting and fun.

Your potential ghostwriter MUST be able to capture your voice and find the true essence of what you want to say in your book. As a new writer working with a ghostwriter, you will depend on your ghostwriter to get the job done. Hiring the perfect ghostwriter involves learning the intricacies of the ghostwriter's possessed skills to generate the best book for you and your readers.

Remember, overall, your relationship with your potential ghostwriter will be a highly collaborative effort, with both you and the writer working together to create the final product. A professional ghostwriter must be able to effectively help you secure the perfect words and vision of your book. And to accomplish this, there must be a strong cooperative effort between you, the author, and the ghostwriter.

Most ghostwriters, as part of their process, conduct author interviews, record the conversation, and transcribe to study your voice, style, and personality. These interviews are usually one-on-one and will involve open interaction, transparency, and boundary-free expectations to avoid any rising conflict or misunderstandings through the process. When both parties, ghostwriter, and author, understand their roles and participates fully, it keeps the book on track and the work flowing.

Ghostwriters and Research for Your Book

Your search for the perfect ghostwriter should require a thorough upfront understanding of any research necessary with your book project. If there is a strong component of research needed with your book's topic, this must be accounted for upfront as part of what you will require of your ghostwriter.

Remember, any additional research, as part of a ghostwriting agreement, will allude to a more substantial fee to compensate the ghostwriter for their time and extra work involved with the research. To help you save time, you should do a preliminary outline of the topics that will need to be researched. The research outline will provide the ghostwriter with a general overview and a better idea of the work required before starting your book.

Searching for the perfect ghostwriter involves many variables you must consider. Vincent Van Gogh once said, *"If I cease searching, then, woe is me, I am lost. That is how I look at it - keep going, keep going, come what may."*

Keep searching, do not settle, and talk to different ghostwriters, ask for writing samples, view their portfolios until you find the one that meets the specific criteria necessary for your book. Searching for the best fitting ghostwriter involves understanding essential factors to get your book project completed. Use these tools I have outlined as a guide and never give up— until the fit is perfect and complete.

Chapter 2/ WHAT Publishing Plan to Take with Your Ghostwriter

"Don't classify me, read me. I'm a writer, not a genre."

— Carlos Fuentes

Strategically Planning Your Book

We have established there are multiple reasons to work with a ghostwriter and defining how the collaboration is going to proceed. The writing of a book involves planning and collaborating with your ghostwriter as an essential step in developing a strategic plan with your book. Your specific plan should start by understanding what type of book you are going to write. There are different genres of books, and only you know where your book fits into the scheme of the book world.

Planning your book is just like planning your business. If you were to start a new business, you would create a business plan to follow to make sure your business stays on track. This is the same as your book. Planning your book keeps you on track, and it allows you to follow the process to help your book be successful.

But when it comes to hiring a ghostwriter, before you do, understanding what type of book you want to write is essential also. The vital aspect of locating the right ghostwriter is having a thorough understanding of your book's topic. The main goal of searching for a ghostwriter is determining how to help the ghost capture the essence of what you do and what your expertise is on the page. All of which will aid in the cost of writing your book. I have discovered the more I know about the scope of a project, the better I can put together a budget-friendly pricing proposal.

For a ghostwriter, understanding if your book needs advanced research or a larger (word count) book size will determine the fee a ghostwriter could potentially charge to write your book. The essential steps in the planning of your book are page count, word count, and research involved. These are crucial factors which are critical first steps in planning your book. Included with these steps involves understanding your genre and where your book's main category will help you in finding the right ghostwriter fit.

Understanding Genres

As you are thinking of hiring a ghostwriter, writing a book includes understanding what specific category your book will fit under. This is critical to get started on the right track because there is a multitude of different genres and interests that many authors write their books under. Yet, the insight of each one is crucial in determining the direction of your book. For the sake of time, I will briefly discuss fiction writing later in the chapter, although I am mainly going to focus on genres of writing nonfiction.

The styles of nonfiction books include but are not limited to:

- Self-help (weight loss, exercise, cooking, time management, goals, etc.)
- Business/Business Management Books
- Memoirs and Biographies
- Autobiography
- Creative Nonfiction
- True Crime
- Spiritual/Religion

Self-Help

Self-help books are undoubtedly one of the most significant market sectors in the publishing industry. Most nonfiction titles consist of self-help books that exist to serve one function, and that is to help the reader by instruction, providing guidance, enlightenment, and or provide alternative perspectives.

Self-help books are exactly as the name suggests. They provide the reader insight into outlying principles within the book that can either elevate, educate, or enhance the reader to improve their lives. Self-help books can give vital information to get a better job, make more money, lose weight, or even how to make pets have a better life. Self-help books address specific problems and provide solutions leading the reader to live a better life.

However, within the self-help book genre, there are also *Perspective books* that are written in a straight-forward style providing simple instructions. These are the kinds of books, for example, if you want to raise your credit score or learn how to shoot a gun. They will show you how exactly the steps you need to take to improve that credit rating or make you a better marksman.

Descriptive perspective books teach everything from exercise, weight loss, weight training to making more money, climbing the corporate ladder, credit, and even trading and the stock market. As an example, this book you are reading can be considered a prescriptive book because its intention is outlining the steps in hiring and working with a ghostwriter. A dead giveaway on finding a prescriptive self-help book are the words "How to" or "Guide," which are often in the title and tell you upfront what you're going to learn inside the book.

The other type of self-help book is called *Aspirational self-help.* In these books, you will find testimonials, case studies, and instruction from people who have improved their lives with the material within the book. They are real-life adaptations of how someone has helped themselves by using their own advice and provide advice to a reader experiencing the same issues. This book can also be described as an aspirational book because I am guiding you with my book writing experience.

This type of book is written by people who have overcome different challenges and desire to show the reader there is hope and ways to overcome these challenges. For example, I am an amputee. I lost my left leg below the knee in 2017, and one of the books I have written, AMPOSSIBLE (*coming 2021 Rowman & Littlefield*), is about learning how to adapt and cope with your life being an amputee. The book is a deep-dive journey into the life of an amputee from the first days to getting your life back. It was written to instill inspiration as it was my true story of when and how I lost my left leg. I wrote the book and applied my story with the intent to use my experience to help every amputee across the world.

Aspirational self-help books provide more generalized or types of influential and even spiritual guidance. Yet, even though they may not describe the specific steps and how to solve a problem, they encourage enlightenment and promote inspiration. Many of the best self-help books offer a combination of instruction and inspiration or an intertwining of the two. Aspirational books could include or involve the story of the author's own rise or first-hand experience within that genre.

Business Management Books

I have written multiple business books for CEOs, entrepreneurs, and Fortune 500 company leaders across the country. I now specialize in writing for business, and I love writing in this genre because I believe these leaders provide a rare and unique insight that many readers would not be able to get any other way. Business is essential to our national economy and the American spirit. These books provide an avenue for any serious business leader and knowledge-seeking reader to come together. Business books open the immense possibility of terrific new businesses being started and developed.

There are many nonfiction books written in the business management sector, and many business books describe how to manage a business, brand recognition, increase business and operate a company, all the while giving the reader specific aspects in doing so. Readers can learn how to manage finances, operate human resources, or even business marketing and advertising. The genre is open and exciting.

Memoirs and Biographies

Many nonfiction books are memoirs and biographies of peoples' lives. There isn't any doubt that readers everywhere find other people's lives fascinating. Books written by celebrities, politicians, musicians, and prolific entities are massively extraordinary and enticing.

If you are here as a high-profile author thinking of writing a memoir and having it ghostwritten, the first aspect to consider is who will want to read your book. Are you a celebrity and believe your life has generated a mystique the general public is interested in? If so, then you might consider getting a deal with a traditional publisher.

Maybe you're not famous but intend to write and publish your life story for your family, friends, and or business associates. Having a book of this nature ghostwritten is an excellent way to present to the world your memoir. Your book will introduce your life's history, never been shown before.

The good news is many books such as these appear on Amazon® and across bookstores around the nation; and, if marketed right— do sell well. A person's private life draws massive interest from readers across the world.

Autobiography

There is a difference between an autobiography and a memoir. An autobiography tells the story of life direct from the author's viewpoint. As an author, if you intend to write an autobiography with a ghostwriter, remember, this will involve developing a close-knit relationship as you will be sharing pertinent and private details of your life. An autobiography involves revealing touchstone events; or what can be considered the turning points from the author's life.

Yet, if you believe your life story needs to be told and put out into the world to read, hiring a ghostwriter could be hugely beneficial for your book. By talking and being open with your ghostwriter, you may experience revelations and discover intricate details about your life you didn't know or had long forgotten about. These essential details could make the difference from an ordinary book to an extraordinarily successful book.

Be mindful and be careful here. Do not let a potential ghostwriter talk you into writing the story and give you false hope in believing that your book will be a bestseller. The reality is simple. Your life is important and exciting, but not everyone's life is worthy of being a bestseller. So, I'm not saying your book and life can't be a best seller (as it very well could be). But, we are discussing hiring a ghostwriter, and any ghostwriter who immediately assures you that your book will be a bestseller is a person that you should try to avoid. Why? ...Because this ghostwriter is not forthcoming and honest with you.

Creative Nonfiction

Creative nonfiction is a genre that has become immensely popular and has, in a sense, morphed over spans of decades into full-length books. Many famous works have been written in the creative nonfiction genre. They are the perfect medium if you have lived a unique experience, desire to put a different spin on a subject, or want to bring to the forefront specific historical events.

Creative nonfiction provides the outlet to bring your story to life and provide an avenue in which you, as the author, can deliver in a uniquely creative way as nonfiction. Famous examples of creative nonfiction can be found in great titles, including:

- Ernest Hemingway, "A Moveable Feast" (1964)
- George Orwell, "Essays" (2002)
- E.B. White, "Essays of E.B. White" (1977)
- Tom Wolfe, "The Right Stuff" (1979)

Books of these statures are ones that are memorable and that have struck a chord with America throughout the ages. Creative nonfiction is a beautiful art form, and this is the type of book that draws the reader into real-life action. If creative nonfiction is the book you would like to write, hiring a professional ghostwriter that specializes in this form of writing is essential.

Writing a creative nonfiction book will involve the close-knit relationship between you and your ghostwriter. Herein lies the reason; I discussed earlier in the book when choosing the right ghostwriter because, in this genre, you will be working closely with your writer for longer durations of time. The right relationship must be there between you and the writer to create a thriving creative nonfiction book.

Fiction

Since you were a child, you have been exposed to fiction books; everything from picture books like *"Goodnight Moon"* By Margaret Wise to *"Where the Wild Things Are"* by Maurice Sendak. And who can forget the J.K. Rowling, *"Harry Potter"* series? Then there are authors as prolific as Stephen King, who dominates the fiction world with stories of haunting, bone-chilling terror. He is in great company with authors like Edgar Allen Poe, Mark Twain, and Ernest Hemingway. What all these authors have in common is years of fiction writing experience.

Writing fiction is an acquired skill filled with a lifetime of learning the craft. So, if you are a fiction writer and have a new provocative book idea you want to share with the world, yet do not possess the necessary skills to write your book, hiring a ghostwriter to create the manuscript for you is indispensable. Be aware you will probably have to prepare an outline or a general idea of the story from the beginning to the end. In fiction, the competition is stiff, and it's challenging to have a story that will attract the attention of a major publisher or a literary agent.

There's an immense amount of work that must be done for your story to rise above the crowd. Before you start, define ways your story will be unique and will attract attention over the competition and grab the interest of a literary agent or major publisher. When you locate and hire your ghostwriter, discuss the details of your fiction book idea, and do everything possible to aid your ghostwriter in creating the fiction book that will find success.

Every book genre has the potential of being a bestseller, and every book has a potential being a bombastic flop. A good ghostwriter should remain positive about your book yet be responsible for informing you of the realities of the marketplace with fiction. The truth is, the publishing industry, as a whole, is intensely competitive, and very few books make a profit. The choice is yours to move forward if your story needs to be told. Only, do yourself a favor and understand the reality.

When I meet with a client, once I discover the type of book the author wants to write, I inform upfront and deliver real-world expectations. I understand, as part of my job, the different markets. Even though I strive earnestly to write the best book I can for every one of my clients, as a professional ghostwriter, I feel it is my job to provide direct and honest ideas and expectations upfront to my authors. Any ghostwriter, worth their salt, should do the same with you.

Phase TWO "WHO"

WHO Needs to Hire a Ghostwriter?

Chapter 3/ WHO Needs to Find and Hire a Ghostwriter?

"Knowing is not understanding. There is a great difference between knowing and understanding: you can know a lot about something and not really understand it."

- Charles Kettering

The only way I know to do any task I have in front of me is to address it head-on. Once there, I work diligently in achieving the task and do everything within my power to do so. However, I know when to give up the reigns and allow other individuals to acquire the task all in the name of making my life easier. Hiring a ghostwriter is precisely the same.

When it comes to ghostwriting, understanding my role within the book writing process is the first step. This understanding is the purpose and is necessary for successful book collaboration. To achieve success in finding and hiring the perfect ghostwriter, you must first know and understand yourself and who you are within the role you play with your book. Yet, the question remains, you need to ask yourself, *"Do I need a ghostwriter for my book?"*

To answer this question, let's first examine and define the roles where you and your book are concerned. Your specific situation is the primary determiner. Perhaps you are the CEO of a large company, and every minute of every day is consumed with necessary and essential tasks to ensure the company's operation remains running smoothly. Many people depend on you to keep the cogs in the wheels turning, and taking time to sit down and write a book is virtually impossible. Are you a hard-working business person? If this describes you, it is safe to say you would be a prime candidate to hire a ghostwriter.

Maybe you are at a point in your life where a significant event has happened to you, and you now want to write a book. Yet, growing up, through school and even college, the writing wasn't something that ever interested you. As a matter of fact, you found it to be quite dull, and you never quite got the hang of it. If this sounds like you, and you are asking yourself (before you even get started), "Would I even enjoy writing a book?" You should highly consider hiring a ghostwriter.

Are you the person who never missed a roll call of attendance in English class, but still do not know an adjective, from a colon? However, writing is something we each do every day with emails, text messages, even letters, yet excellent, professional, highly-skilled writing takes years to achieve— even to reach satisfactory results. Author Virginia Woolf, in her book, *Orlando*, wrote, *"For once the disease of reading has laid hold upon the system, it weakens it so that it falls an easy prey to that other scourge which dwells in the inkpot and festers in the quill. The wretch takes to writing."* This raises an honest question of whether you have the talent or disposition to write an entire book. *Do you?* Give yourself an authentic assessment, and if the answer is no, then hiring a ghostwriter is the perfect route to take with your book.

Perhaps you recognize the fact that you do not possess the ability to sit for long hours, undistracted, and unencumbered to write a book. A writer must be able to be self-driven and self-motivated every single day. A professional writer doesn't need a boss to crack the whip or ring a bell to start and stop work. Work begins, and once it does, the attention must never wane from the book's objective. There is a sacrifice necessary for writing a book. It is a selfless act, so, in essence, do you have the discipline to write your book? If you are frank with yourself and earnestly recognize that you are not disciplined enough—don't start a book. Instead, hire a professional ghostwriter to see it through.

Possibly you have decided to write your book, and your hectic schedule precludes you from performing thorough research and interviews your book needs. Some books, and most nonfiction works, even children's books take an immense amount of research to accomplish. The facts must be checked and double-checked. If you are honest with yourself and recognize you do not have the bandwidth or the ability to perform professional research and fact-checking for your book, hiring a ghostwriter is the practical answer.

Writing a book is an incredibly significant decision and a huge undertaking. As a new author, if you are authentic with yourself and any of these scenarios are a real-life depiction of you, you are WHO I would advise hiring a ghostwriter. Ghostwriting is considered a professional service, much like any other service in the world. When you need a plumber, you call a plumber. When you need your vehicle repaired, you take it to an auto mechanic. Your book is the same. Can't do the work—hire a ghostwriter.

If you want or need a book written and you don't possess any of these traits listed above, you need to consider seriously hiring a ghostwriter. There isn't any shame in recognizing and admitting the need to hire a professional ghostwriting service to accomplish your book. Get past the stigma and get going with your book.

Phase 3 "WHY"

WHY You Need to Hire a Ghostwriter

Chapter 4/ Deciding "WHY" to Hire a Ghostwriter

"If there is one sweeping generalization I can make without fear of contradiction, it is that 'change' is the scariest word in the English language Nothing will change in our lives until we change our own behavior. Insight won't do it. Understanding why we do the self-defeating things we do won't make us stop doing them. Nagging and pleading with the other person to change won't do it. We have to act. We have to take the first step down a new road."

~ *Susan Forward*

We have all seen them over and over, yet most of the time, we don't even give them a second glance. I know I never did, but now that we are discussing the work of professional ghostwriters, I am drawn to them. What I am referring to is the secondary name present on a book's cover with the author's—the ghostwriter. I can't help myself to scan the cover of a book, looking for the name of the author and the ghostwriter. What I am talking about is the little "with" and the "and" below an author's name.

All the little "with" and "and" all represent the input of a ghostwriter or collaborator— who physically wrote the book. Almost every CEO, celebrity, and hectic business person have seen the need to utilize their time and employ the skill of a professional ghostwriter to write their books. For many CEOs, a ghostwritten book saves time, vast amounts of money, and has proven to be the quickest route for favorable publicity.

Writing a book is still held in the highest regard, even though self-publishing and traditional publishing have opened the doors wide to many getting into the book-writing game. A book is still an honor, a symbol of prestige, and hiring a ghostwriter to pen it is seen as a mere tool to accomplish an author's dream.

A book can be written as a business memoir or a personal memoir of a CEO or celebrity's life. Most large corporations have seen the need for the founder to write a book to help the company with increased media engagement, customer acquisition, building a brand, strengthen a reputation, or to aid in replenishing a bad one.

I had a new author come to me, gung-ho and ready to get out of the gate with his new book. We had contracts signed and everything in place. The writing began, and everything was going superb. One afternoon, he reached out with a concern. "Jeff," he said, "I have been hearing from a lot of my colleagues. They tell me I should NOT put your name on the cover with mine. I am being told many readers don't like to see the ghostwriter's name on the cover. I think it makes me look like a fraud."

Admittedly, I was taken aback for a second because he and I were under contract, which stated, *"Giving me writing credit on the cover."* I explained to him that many famous celebrities, political figures, and CEOs have all used ghostwriters, and their books went on to sell thousands—even millions of books. Donald Trump, Bill Clinton, Dr. Ben Carson, to name a few, all used ghostwriters. Each of these distinguished men made no qualms and placed their ghostwriter's name on the covers of their books. Their readers didn't mind seeing the ghostwriter's name on the cover other than the author.

Why? Because most people understand that even though there is a ghostwriter, the story, the information, the ideas are straight from the author. The ghostwriter is merely a vessel in getting these aspects onto the page. Even though my author was insistent on removing my name from his cover, the work was still ghostwritten by me; the words, stories, and ideas were all from him, the author. However, when it came to the general reading public, it didn't make a difference one way or the other.

Ghostwriting Stigma

One crucial aspect is overcoming the stigma of hiring a ghostwriter. This seems to be a hot topic as many new authors have an initial problem with the perception of having a ghostwriter's name credited or associated with their work. Many do not wish for their potential readers to think the author themselves didn't write the book.

Kevin Anderson, CEO of Kevin Anderson & Associates, explains in his article for Northshore magazine, *"But the fact of the matter is, the author really is the author. We're* [ghostwriters] *just a very sophisticated pen. It's the author's idea, their message, and their stories."*

Ghostwriting a book from an author and ghostwriter's standpoint is entirely organic and authentic. Although some strongly disagree, nevertheless, having a book ghostwritten can hardly be described as not authentic because ghostwriting an author's book requires both author and ghostwriter to engage in a deep one-on-one writing relationship, sharing original, and confidential material.

During this process, intricate details are shared by the author and ghostwriter. (Hence, why you need to find a writer you get along with well.) The ghostwriter's job is to write the words, capture emotions, harness the nuance of the author's words and thoughts onto the page. A ghostwriter, a good one, can deliver these deep-rooted thoughts, experiences, and skills in the author's voice, tone, and style. Even though a ghostwriter does the physical writing, the relationship between ghost and author involves sharing personal insight directly from the author, and it requires compatibility between all parties to capture tone, style, and voice.

When I ghostwrite a book, I earnestly strive to find my client's voice. I listen intently, study, and research my author's interviews for specific dialects, phrases, words used, and patterns. I depict essential facts and information from transcripts, along with familiarizing myself with speech patterns and mannerisms that capture the nuance of every author. Then I put all of this together and build the book with these unique pieces and focus solely on the author's message using these newfound tools. A good ghostwriter MUST be able to accomplish this with your book. If you hire a ghostwriter and they cannot capture your voice and message—don't waste time and move on—find one that can.

The WHY in Hiring a Ghostwriter

There is a multitude of reasons for new authors to write a book with a ghostwriter. Today, in our society, with the hectic pace of the business world, Most CEOs and business entities are busy performing their day-to-day work roles.

These jobs, being chaotic and fast-paced, do not leave time, in most of these people's schedules to sit down for six to nine months, and put pen to paper and write a book. Savvy CEOs, corporate leaders, celebrities, musicians, artists, and small and large companies now recognize that their time is money, and hiring a professional ghostwriter is the most practical solution in getting a book written.

Every book starts with a dream, desire, and a goal, along with a deep understanding of the WHY to write a book. Knowing the direct reason for what you are looking to accomplish with your book is essential. Realizing your book's direction is a crucial step when starting your search for a ghostwriter.

- ***What is your REASON for writing a book?***
- ***What are you looking for and need in a ghostwriter?***

Maybe you have tried to sit down and draft a book of your own. Yet, halfway through you realized, you need help. Or perhaps you have extensive knowledge on a specific subject and possess unique skills that you want to share with the world— but don't know how to convey your message in words. You are not alone, as many top industry leaders, Fortune 500 company execs, celebrities, CEOs, and small business owners have found themselves in these same positions— and most decided to pursue using a ghostwriter.

Level and Experience of the Ghostwriter

Finding the professional ghostwriter that fits with your personality and book goals is vital. Start by asking yourself what level of experience and expertise you are looking for. Are you trying to save money and hire a part-time writer? Are you willing to give a newbie a shot? Or are you looking for someone with defined skills with vast experience in your field? If so, these specialized skills come at a price.

I have written for major 'Big-Five' publishers, including Harper Collins®, Harper Collins Leadership®, Rowman & Littlefield®, Highbridge Audio®, and Audible®. Along with that, I have written books for top CEOs, and every project pushed me to work diligently and sharpen my skills to be at the top of my writing game. Plus, it propelled me to hone my craft, study, and rise above the crowd by being professional at every level with my skills and writing etiquette.

I recognize, as most professional ghostwriters, that most Fortune 500 executives expect to hire the best and are not comfortable leaving their book, their message, and their knowledge in the hands of a novice writer. If you are a CEO or industry leader and budget is not a concern, I advise you to seek out competent, highly skilled ghostwriters with correlating experience to your expectations and industry. I suggest choosing a writer who has more than one book to their writing credit.

But if you own a small business and must worry about the budget, do your best to choose a ghostwriter who meshes with your ideals and book project while remaining friendly on your budget. This is a fine-edged sword to contend with. New writers will have new skills yet, lack the experience of the publishing industry. Remember, in most instances, less skill level equals a lower budget. High-level skills, professional writing credentials, and expertise most always equal higher cost. These formulas are the way of the ghostwriting world.

However, beware and avoid the lure of the bottom basement writing deals. In the end, you will not come out with the quality writing and book you need to be successful. Don't get me wrong; there are many good writers out there that are new and just starting, yet there are some who are downright mediocre, and their fees reflect their skills. Do not waste your time.

Most top industry leaders, CEOs, and celebrities, even small business owners, demand a certain level of professionalism and experience a ghostwriter must possess to make their book a success. Understanding this begins with knowing what you want to accomplish with your book, and what stage your book is currently in.

Industry leaders know hiring a skilled professional ghostwriter is the only way to get the job done right. And the savvy leaders of today enjoy saving time and money by hiring a ghostwriter. Mind you, hiring a writer that doesn't have credits, a strong portfolio, or has never worked in your industry could be an ingredient for disaster.

The good news is you do not have to be a tremendous industry leader in finding and hiring the caliber of ghostwriting talent you need to help make your book a success. Being an author, on any level, recognizing your strengths and weaknesses is the mark of a true professional. Using a high caliber sought-after ghostwriter will provide you with top-quality writing and stress-free experience you deserve.

Hiring a ghostwriter is an immense step toward your future, and I applaud you for being sharp, open-minded, and humble enough to admit that there are significant reasons you can't write a marketable manuscript. And this is the reason why many business people, CEOs, and industry leaders choose the ghostwriting route, because of these very same reasons.

Many extraordinarily successful people understand the benefits of having a book, and the benefits of sharing their life stories, experiences, or skills with the public. Having a book brings the author clout and a distinguished form of notoriety. If influence, notoriety, and a superior book dream have you seeking a polished professional manuscript, hiring an experienced ghostwriter is the route you need to take— and one you will never regret.

As a professional ghostwriter, I understand the full intensive ghostwriting game. I write the words, but the work belongs solely to the author, and my job is to bring the author's experience and stories to the page. Along the way, the author and I become collaborators or co-creators. But the written work belongs to the authors.

I know my role and my stance, and I believe that every professional ghostwriter must (and does) understand their position. A good ghostwriter will recognize how they interplay with you in writing your book and maintain that throughout the writing process.

My intent is for my ghostwriting clients to walk away, feeling as if they had typed every word; the only variance— I did the physical writing and saved them countless hours by allowing the author to avoid the writing process. Most CEOs and business entities are tremendously busy performing their day to day work roles. All of which does not afford extra time in their schedules to sit down for six-nine months and put pen to paper and write a book. This is the reason many savvy CEOs, corporate leaders, celebrities, musicians, artists, and companies around the globe have recognized that time is money, and hiring a professional ghostwriter is essential in getting the book written.

Ernest Hemingway wrote, *"It's none of their business that you have to learn to write. Let them think you were born that way."* So, once you're past the stigma of hiring a ghostwriter, there must be an understanding of the economic business standpoint involved in using a ghostwriter. A ghostwriter's job is the same as any other service job. It is the same reason Steve Jobs, Donald Trump, Michael Jordan, or Bill Clinton don't cut their own grass. Their time, just like your time, is worth money, and it is not economically feasible to stop, take a few months off to write a book, and take a disastrous financial hit to their income.

Jerry Jenkins, President of The Jenkins Group, a book publishing firm, was quoted in a recent article written in Priceonomics by Alex Mayyasi. Mr. Jenkins said, *"The appeal is pretty clear, if you are an executive making $10 million a year, will you really stop working for two to three months to write a book? Or if you're an athlete?"* This raises a distressing question. If you are making this kind of money, could you afford to stop, take time out, and write a book? The answer—probably not.

The WHY Reason to Write Your Book

Madeleine L'Engle once wrote, *"You have to write the book that wants to be written. And if the book will be too difficult for grown-ups, then you write it for children."* No matter what type of book you intend to write, everyone has the specific reasons they want to produce a book for the world to read. While searching for your ghostwriter, explore the deep insights into the main reasons for your book. It is imperative to understand one hundred percent of your "WHY" for writing your book. The WHY of your book, I believe, derives from deep soul searching not only of the subject, but of yourself, and by projecting the innermost thoughts on the subject out loud.

I know first-hand that writing a book is a momentous decision in your life. I have written many books for myself, and every single one of them was undoubted and had a specified direction. Each book was a significant decision in which I knew EXACTLY what I wanted to say and WHY I was saying it. Not one of them was written without a complete understanding of WHY I was writing the book. This is essential for you to do the same.

As a professional ghostwriter, part of my job is peeling back the layers and helping each author understand their WHY. I accomplish this by answering pertinent questions I receive from many new authors. I encourage everyone to ask questions and recognize every question is of great importance. I never answer any question lightly and tackle each question as I do each book— by addressing each one— with vigor.

Most of the time, these are the most prominent, "break-the-ice" questions I receive. Questions such as:

- *How much does it cost to write a book?*
- *How do you write in my voice?*

Even the most basic questions cannot be answered appropriately unless I know a few things about you and your book. So, to give a new author the best possible and fair answer, I ask one vitally important question that goes back to the significant point of —knowing your WHY.
"Why do you want to write a book?"

Yes, I know that may sound like the simplest of questions with seemingly the most elementary of answers, but I assure you—it is not. For an author to answer this accurately, they must be willing, or, at the very least, take the opportunity to look deeper within themselves. Realizing the profound reason, you want to write a book is critical in not only the pursuit of writing the book but the execution of a solid plan to hiring your ghostwriter. I guess you can say, "the rubber hits the road" at this juncture. Let me ask you— have you assessed the primary purpose and asked yourself this question? Have you examined your intentions for your book deeply?

If not—stop now— and do so.

One of the first premises to writing any book is you need to have something you want to say to the world. Everyone has that one factor that defines them as a person, individual, husband, father, or corporate leader. What is the reason that gets you out of bed each day? What excites you and drives your passion for spreading the word to the world? It is up to you to figure out what it "IS" that you want to say. Once you do, understand it will help you in finding the right ghostwriter for your project. Here are a few questions to ask yourself to help you determine the WHY before you hire your ghostwriter and write your book:

- What is the book's main subject?
- What is the book's main style?
- What are the book's main points?
- What is the book's primary goal? (Your goals)

- Who is the book's primary reader? (Target Audience)
- How much research will be necessary and expected with the ghostwriter?

Answering these critical questions will get you on the right track when starting to talk to potential ghostwriters. Once you understand the WHY and what it IS you want to say, the next idea is to understand your primary reader fully. It is essential to know so, ask yourself who the person or group of people is that are going to read it. Who is your main reader, and what will they get out of reading it?

To hire your perfect ghostwriter, and to put your book on the right path, you will need to define YOUR MAIN TARGET READER. Without this understanding, the book will float aimlessly around and not see much success. Make this your mission to narrow down on your book's focus; to capture a specific audience. Examining the main reasons for all of this may sound elementary, but I warn you, this step should never be overlooked. The benefit of knowing your book, the why, and who the primary reader is will help you to understand your motives for writing your book. So, here are various reasons to write your book:

Residual Income

Maybe you want to have a book that will support your existing business by providing residual income. A book can do this for sure. If this is your main reason, understand there will be specific processes necessary to be put into place.

For a book to produce residual income, you will need to know your primary target reader. Depending on what business or intent, your target audience could include: consumers, business to business, and or companies. Defining who reads your book will potentially skyrocket your sales and allow you to bring in significant residual income. Plus, knowing you are pursuing residual income will help you locate the ghostwriter most skilled in helping you accomplish and implement to reach the income stream you are hoping for.

Support Your Speaking Engagements

Are you a professional speaker? Maybe you desire to support your speaking engagements by writing a book to promote your services and present your knowledge on your subject in written form. A book of this nature is great to have for what is called "Backroom Sales." These books can also promote additional speaking engagements and, in turn, make you and your business more profitable.

Tell Your Unique Story

Do you have a unique story to tell? Have you experienced something or gone through something that could help others? Writing a book is an excellent way to share with the world the story and have possibly millions share in your story.

Help Others

Do you have a specific skill or knowledge on a subject that can help others and solve their problems? Writing a book is an excellent way to accomplish that and generate sales. Setting out to write a book of this nature will solidify your intent to help others and solve their problems through your words. Understanding this will help you find the ghostwriter best suited for this purpose.

Promote Your Business

Do you want to write a book to help promote your skills or services? Having a book that supports your business can be perceived as a long-term business card that will lead to new clients. Plus, a book will aid in reinforcement that you are the leader in your field. A book will help increase your income and bottom line. Find the ghostwriter skilled in writing for business.

Lead Generation

Are you thinking of having a book as an extended version of your business to help you generate leads? To accomplish this, your book must be perceived as a long-term plan to generate increased leads from your website. If you plan to use your book as a lead magnet, prepare to give it away as a download or give a portion of the book in exchange for a potential client's email address. Hire the ghostwriter who understands business-to-business and has the skills to write in that style.

The many immense benefits of writing a book, whatever direction you choose, will drastically impact your life. Writing a book is a choice of a lifetime and is an element that must be addressed from deep within you. Use these tools, your drive, and your passion to search for and hire the perfect ghostwriter for your book.

Phase 4 "WHEN"

WHEN to Hire and Work with a Ghostwriter

Chapter 5/ Knowing "When" to Hire a Ghostwriter

"People are not your most important asset. The right people are."

– Jim Collins

Your journey in searching for your perfect ghostwriter not only begins with understanding WHY you need to hire a writer but involves a necessary understanding of WHEN you need to find one. Knowing when to hire a ghostwriter is as critical as to the "why" for various reasons. The WHEN is, in a sense, a reckoning. Knowing WHEN comes from a deep understanding of your life and your time as a critical ending asset—that you don't have any to spare. And, yet, the book you intend to write has intrinsic value because you have reached a point where your busy life has intersected with the dream of writing a book. Now, you are in a situation where there is not a way to ignore the pull or fascination— and the time is now to get started.

As a business person, there is a multitude of reasons for considering collaborating with a ghostwriter. It could begin with something as simple as following your dream of writing a book or your company needs a breath of fresh air and a new approach to marketing your services. Nonetheless, if other vital reasons are evident— evaluating WHEN is essential.

Not Enough Time

If you have seen or felt the influence to write a book and have decided it is time, yet you do not have the luxury of extra time, then now is the perfect opportunity to get it done. Whether you are a CEO of a Fortune 500 company or a small business owner, time, along with company and family responsibilities, makes it challenging and near impossible to have the extra time to sit down and write your book. If this is you, collaborating with a ghostwriter is the essential answer. Working with a professional ghostwriter allows you to remain in your life, maintain your business, and spend time with those who count the most. Plus, enjoy the journey knowing your book is finally being written.

Tried Writing But Failed

Dave G., a past author client, and good friend, told me his story. "I woke up one morning, and I had the urge to sit down and write my book. Man, I've seen it a hundred times on television. You know, writers sitting down in front of their laptop and begin writing. It looked easy, so I decided I wanted to do it. But when I did, it didn't take long for me to find out— it is not easy! And Jeff, this led me to search and find you."

Does Dave's story sound familiar? Have you ever felt like Dave? Maybe you've sat down and attempted to put words on paper (or computer these days), but it came out wrong, strangely, or perhaps not at all. If this describes you, trust me, you are not alone. Most people go through this only to discover the difficulties in writing a book. If you are one of those people, then now is the time to collaborate with a ghostwriter.

Not Up to Professional Standards

Every day, I speak to many new author clients, and what I find most of the time is many people have written their manuscripts up to a certain point. Some even have a fully completed manuscript, assessed their work honestly, and have realized the manuscript is not up to professional standards, and they need some help. Hiring a ghostwriter is the answer to taking the manuscript from its current condition and pushing it toward a bestseller status.

A professional ghostwriter should possess the skills to take your existing manuscript, work the words, and produce the necessary "magic" to take your manuscript to the next level. I call this ghostwriting work, *"Book Doctoring."* Humbling yourself and recognizing the need to make your manuscript better is a giant leap forward to your book's success. Author Daphne Rose Kingma said, *"Holding on is believing that there's a past; letting go is knowing that there's a future."* Prolific German Author Herman Hesse said it best, *"Some of us think holding on makes us strong, but sometimes it is letting go."*

Letting go of the control to take your manuscript to the next level because it does not meet your high expectations is a monumental step. I recently wrote a memoir for a new author Perry J. When Perry came to me, she had written the entire manuscript. Yet, she humbly recognized that her work needed help. I stepped in and together, she and I wrote a fantastic new book. Hiring a professional ghostwriter is one of the smartest moves you can make because there are millions of books around the world, and it takes skill, passion, and a never-ending drive for your book to stand out and reach the top to become a bestseller.

Need a Professional Who Knows the Market

James Caan is chairman of the Start-Up-Loans-Company®. In his article for The Guardian®, he wrote, "Everybody always says that knowing your market is everything. Saying it is one thing, but understanding why it is so important will help you stay ahead of the pack. Your market includes your customers, your suppliers, and your competitors – to name a few. But these three are pivotal characters that define the success of your business. Obviously, your customers are the ones buying from your business. Getting to know what they like, how much they will spend, what they enjoy, and what they will give you a better understanding of what they will want from you, enabling you to translate your product into something that will sell to your target market." [i]

In this excerpt, Mr. Caan wrote candidly about knowing your market and who you will direct your marketing towards. It is essential to understand a book is a business, and it is your business. By writing your book, you will be creating a product that needs to be sold. And to sell a product, you must understand your market.

Herein shows the essential need in hiring a professional who comprehends your market, and industry, and attempts to breathe much-needed life into your manuscript. A professional ghostwriter should be able to help you define your target reader and narrow the focus of your book to attract those target readers. Without intent and focus, the manuscript would be what sailors say "lost at sea."

Seeking Long-Term Book Success

Long-term success is something I believe we all strive for, only on different levels. We all have different definitions of what success looks like. Having a roof over your head and food on the table may be a success to some, and then others believe, millions in the bank, big houses, and caviar is the only way to call themselves successful.

The late Robin Leach®, the television talk show host of The Lifestyles Rich and Famous®, once described success by saying, "Never give up if you really want something, keep plugging away at it, and your dreams can come true." Mr. Leach was also noted in saying, "I'm convinced that if the same opportunities were made available to everybody, people would want to better their lot in life."

I believe Mr. Leach was right on all counts. If everyone had the same opportunities as others, some people might be further in life. The beautiful part of writing a book is that the playing field is level, and you, the author, possess the same opportunity as everyone else to achieve success with your book. The critical factor here is it is up to you to rise above and write a manuscript that stands the test of time.

Hiring a professional ghostwriter is a vital step in the process because if you dream of having long-term success with your book, a ghostwriter can take it to the next level. If you seek long-term success with your book, knowing when to hire a ghostwriter, plus how much you believe in yourself— is critical to the equation. If you want to live life and write a bestselling novel and reach the New York Times® bestselling list, hiring a bestselling ghostwriter that possesses the skills in doing so is essential.

A ghostwriter is necessary (if you don't have the writing skills or know-how) and must be hired to draft a bestselling manuscript to improve your chances for long-term success, provide significant income, prestige, and notoriety, throughout your life, in the long term. The critical aspect to all of this, once again, is knowing when to hire a ghostwriter. And it all falls back on the question of WHY?

A book can provide legitimate income and longevity; however, to achieve any notable success, the book must be written professionally, with the mindset of having a bestseller and reaching the bestselling list. To accomplish this, the first step is seeking a ghostwriter who has the skills to achieve and write a professional manuscript worthy of your expectations. The ghostwriter must possess strong enough skills to meet your vision of long-term success with your book. Search and interview ghostwriters who have the experience, along with bestselling titles to their credit. Most importantly, review their work to see if it matches with your style, plan, and expectations.

Be an Expert in Your Field

Has your business grown, yet, you are that one critical stage where you need to increase business? If this is you, writing a book should be the route to pursue. A book is a vital factor in depicting you as an expert in your field— and giving you an edge.

Writing a book with a professional ghostwriter is the answer to gaining that much-needed edge over your competition and increase business. Building your business involves elevating your brand and credibility, and not only can a book increase credibility to new heights, but it will simultaneously raise your sphere of influence and make you the authority in your arena of interest.

To grow your business with a book, hiring a professional ghostwriter is essential to write a marketable and credible manuscript if you intend to declare being an expert in your field.

Vignette – Being, an Expert

> *The Oxford Dictionary and Wikipedia describe the following: An **expert** is someone who has a broad and in-depth competence in terms of knowledge, skill, and experience through practice and education in a particular field. Informally, an expert is someone widely recognized as a reliable source of technique or skill whose faculty for judging or deciding rightly, justly, or wisely is accorded authority and status by peers or the public in a specific well-distinguished domain.*

Take the Stress and Uncertainty

Perhaps you have written some of your book, but you know that your book is not up to the professional level it needs to be for it to be successful. If you have recognized this, then hiring a ghostwriter is the answer. A good ghostwriter should be able to help in relieving your feelings of uncertainty about your manuscript.

Not knowing if you have a manuscript worthy of publication can fill you with stress and can be overwhelming for a new author. Hiring a ghostwriter will enable you to structure your book in the way necessary to reach a saleable, marketable, and professional level.

Knowing when it is time to hire a ghostwriter is essential in your book writing journey. Be proud because just humbling yourself and recognizing you need help is a monumental step— and one you will be pleased to know you did.

Phase 5 "Where"

WHERE to Find and Hire a Ghostwriter

Chapter 6/ Knowing "Where" to Find and Hire the "Write" Ghostwriter

"The secret of my success is that we have gone to exceptional lengths to hire the best people in the world."

~Steve Jobs

We have established that you need at this phase to know the WHY and WHEN of writing your book. The next logical course is locating the perfect ghostwriter for your project. Where do you begin your search? Just like millions of other people each day, one of the best places to start is by performing a thorough Google® search. It is the number one place to start searching and get you going in the right direction.

Before you start your search, compile a list of specified keywords centered on your book's topic to begin your search, for example, ghostwriters of finance, ghostwriters for memoirs, or business ghostwriters. Whatever category best fits your book situation, use those keywords, and see what you find.

After your search, compile a shortlist of the ghostwriters you are most interested in connecting with. Study their websites, blogs, articles, books, and "About" pages. Once there, locate and review any credentials and any portfolios offered. This may take a little time to determine but will be well worth the effort.

The hope with your search is to find the ghostwriter that you believe will match you on a personal level and one you feel you could get along with for a long duration. Lastly, you want to find a writer who has the necessary skills to help you with your book goals.

Ghostwriting Associations

Researching different ghostwriters through professional organizations is a direct way to locate professionals with credentials. The benefits of searching within these organizations are that most of the ghostwriters in these organizations have taken the necessary steps to become a professional.

Within these organizations, you find professional ghostwriters of varying experience. There will be some with multiple writing credits to their names, along with an assortment of newly established writers. And here, most will possess the exceptional skills that you are looking for. There are various organizations, including: The Association of Ghostwriters® (associationofghostwriters.org) and Nonfiction Writers Association® (Nonfictionauthorsassociation.com).

As part of your vetting of ghostwriters, include finding national and local writing associations for prospects. Inquire about your book's project scope and if any suggested ghostwriters may fit the project.

Writing Groups

In your area, you may find dedicated writing groups or associations. Contact your local Secretary of State and ask about any official writing groups in your area. You may also query the internet (Google® and other search engines) and search for writing groups, forums, and even chatrooms. However, be aware as these are some of the places you will find your "discount writers." Use caution, discretion, and common sense when participating in these forums or chats.

Ghostwriters on Reedsy®

Reedsy® is a writer and professional ghostwriter mecca that is dedicated to authors of all levels and publishers. Reedsy® is an essential place to find professional writers for your book. It is one of the unique platforms where writers must have a certain amount of published works (I think currently it is five) in their portfolio before the writer's profile can be seen publicly.

I like this for myself, and for new authors, this provides reassurance that there is a point of entry in place. Not just anyone that claims they are a writer can be seen or become a member. This factor alone separates Reedsy® from the rest of the pack, and for you as a new author allows you to target specific writers in your area of expertise. And Reedsy® offers a fantastic blog helping new writers and authors with publishing and all the learning curves involved in and around the publishing industry. Reedsy® is a leader in providing new tools for new authors to learn about the craft of writing.

Ghostwriters on LinkedIn®

LinkedIn® has fast become one of the essential tools to have in business. Microsoft® reported that LinkedIn's revenue grew 24% in Q2 of 2020 and has currently grown its audience to over 675 million monthly users.[ii] You can research and find different ghostwriting professionals in your specific target area of expertise.

LinkedIn® is a strong leader in connecting business people to other business people. The platform allows you as a new author to use keywords just like you would in Google® or any type of search engine search to find a particular ghostwriter that has written in your area or field.

Start a LinkedIn® account and begin your search. Compile your list and then inquire about the potential ghostwriter by setting up a meeting to talk about your book. LinkedIn® should be an essential part of your initial research in finding your perfect ghostwriter.

Ghostwriters on Upwork®

I couldn't finish out this chapter without mentioning the website Upwork.com®. This is a site where freelancers can place their ads for people searching for freelancers to do work for them, such as writing a book. The only downfall to Upwork® is that anyone can place an ad and listing. There is no official port of entry with Upwork® compared to Reedsy®. Anyone can hang their shingle, declaring they are a writer and join the Upwork® website. And here is where you must proceed with caution. Anyone can claim they are a ghostwriter and never have obtained real writing credentials.

I may receive backlash from successful ghostwriters who started there, and some may even still have an Upwork® listing in place, yet, the truth is the site is now filled with lower budget writers. However, Upwork® is an accessible workplace for jobs where employers or anyone that needs something done can place their requirement for potential freelancers to bid upon. It is a viable resource and worth evaluating when trying to find a ghostwriter that fits your style for your book.

Make sure you know what your project will entail, whether you intend to write a blog or maybe even a shorter eBook; this site may work for you. However, once again, I heed this warning. Upwork® is another area to find writers, but the caliber and quality of the writer must be thoroughly vetted. You must discern and use your best judgment, dependent on your project goals, on whether the ghostwriter will be able to do the work efficiently.

So yes, you will discover discount writers within the platform, and your search for a ghostwriter within Upwork™ could be more challenging in finding one that has the expertise required for your book. Just be aware and use your discretion. If you feel or notice any red flags within your search, then immediately step away, move on, and find another writer.

Phase 6 "How"

HOW to Find and Utilize the Perfect Ghostwriter

Chapter 7/ How to See the Red Flags in Ghost Hunting

"If something on the inside is telling you that someone isn't right for you, they're NOT right for you, no matter how great they might look on paper. When it's right for you, you will know. And when it's not – it's time to go."

— Mandy Hale, The Single Woman: Life, Love, and a Dash of Sass

Since the whole book is about finding the right ghostwriter for your book, I thought it necessary to reveal what is behind the curtain on ghostwriters. (*WARNING- Ghostwriters, I am telling the secrets you may not want most people to know.*) When searching for the right ghostwriter, you must understand what to be on the lookout for to protect you and save you vast amounts of time.

Allow me to say that I belong to many incredible ghostwriting professional organizations filled with real top-level professionals. Many of which, I hope, do understand the honesty I plan to deliver in the next few paragraphs, as I shed light on the many unscrupulous ghostwriting practices in the market.

Ghostwriting is a lucrative profession, yet it is one that lacks a formal point of entry. Much like many other industries, such as innovation, and copywriting ghostwriting, unfortunately, and comparably, does not have an official licensing entity or governing body that enforces entry into the profession. Anyone who has a notion that they want to be a ghostwriter— can enter the game and regrettably without required licensing or certification necessary for entry into the profession. The gateway is "open," unregulated, and anyone can hang their shingle and declare, *"I am Ghostwriter!"*

However, true professionals do place themselves into schools and curriculums to learn the craft and proudly display their certificates of accomplishment. Unfortunately, the lure of making vast amounts of money in the ghostwriting field entices many new rookie ghostwriters to jump right in with both feet. Making big dollars is the drive for many, and most neglect increasing their experience and skills within the industry.

For you, as a new author, this is dangerous territory and where the problem lies. Because you need a ghostwriter who has experience and expertise under their belt. Albert

Einstein said it best, *"Information is not knowledge. The only source of knowledge is experience. You need experience to gain wisdom."*

Your book deserves a professional who has been through the "trials by fire" and knows the industry and possesses the necessary palatable skills. Would you go to a surgeon for back surgery who acquired his skills by reading a few books and articles online? Of course, you wouldn't. You need a writer who has taken it upon themselves the responsibility and respect to become a reputable, experienced writer. For you and your book, the ghostwriter's experience, skills, and publishing expertise are vital to make your book a potential success.

As I stated, ghostwriting is a profession with an apparent "open doors" policy, and gaining knowledge and experience is strictly voluntary. Yet, any ghostwriter worth their salt, who has their morals in the right place, does what is necessary to perfect their craft and uphold the standards of the profession.

Myself, I went through three different ghostwriting curriculums with some of the nation's top ghostwriting courses and instructors. I was mentored by one of the best ghostwriters (and still am) in the business. He has ghostwritten over thirty books, and he has taught me how to be a professional writer from many advantageous viewpoints.

I have another mentor friend who is also my literary agent and professional ghostwriter. My agent has been in the publishing industry in different capacities such as editor, ghostwriter, for over thirty-five years. I respect his opinion, and my work has had to pass under his strict and experienced tutelage. These high standards have made me a better writer, and I am thankful for the opportunity and experience.

Nevertheless, after ghostwriting a few early books, I found out that ghostwriting takes more than study in school. It takes time behind the keyboard and a hell of a lot of hard work. Ghostwriting takes showing up, dedication, and the willingness to acquire hands-on experience and the commitment to work hard, make mistakes, and still build a catalog of different books and eBooks. A good writer (your ghostwriter) must have battle scars and the written work to prove it.

Now, I am not saying you can't find a good ghostwriter that doesn't have a strong portfolio and is just starting out—because you can. How you choose and who you choose is up to you, but just be aware that lack of experience may play into different factors down the road as far as quality, time, and cost.

I understand everyone starts somewhere. I did when I started writing blogs and doing copywriting, not only for myself but for my real estate companies and other companies over the years. Additionally, I have worked for different marketing agencies around the country, honing my skills by writing hundreds of blogs and websites, and I did it all as a ghostwriter. Today, those blogs and sites are active, and no one knows the difference. Only I know that I wrote them (and the agency).

When I was starting out, I worked for one marketing agency (name withheld) that piled on the work and gave me an almost impossible workload itinerary of blogs and webpages that would make any writer's head spin. The work paid next to nothing, and I was getting paid chump change, and I knew it. Yet, I sacrificed myself to hone my craft, and I hit the work head-on.

As I progressed, I was proud that I never missed a deadline—not once. On most of the work, I was ahead of schedule, with minimal revisions. I took on the work understanding I needed to give myself the challenge to perfect my writing skills, meet deadlines, and develop my skills in learning how to write in another person's voice. I met the challenge of delivering strong marketable copy on time, got paid to write, and set myself on the course to be a professional ghostwriter.

My words began to have an impact. It brought in new clients, increased brand awareness, and helped generate significant profits for the agency. It was a good feeling to know this was paid on-the-job training— at its best. I was getting paid (extraordinarily little) to write words to help someone else in their life. Once I discovered this glorious fact and started ghostwriting books for new authors— I have never looked back. I was hooked and wanted to know and learn all that I could about the profession.

...Yet, not all writers are like me.

Many enter into the ghostwriting arena with only dollar signs in their eyes. I feel I must say (out of fairness and transparency) that the ghostwriting profession is filled with scammers and want-to-be's, all out to separate you from your dollar and never deliver what you need as far as a substantial manuscript. Their main concern is their wallet and not the quality or outcome of your project. Be aware and do not get sucked into low-cost, less skilled ghostwriters. Yes, you can find them. They are out there in droves, but if you want to have a book experience worthy of your life, skills, and expertise, stop picking the low hanging fruit and go for the top.

Simply put, be prepared, save, and find the best writer that fits you and your budget. The reality is the ghostwriting industry does not have any formal standard of entry or ethics. Much like the Bat-Signal® over Gotham City, most newly so-called ghostwriters see the beacon call of the almighty dollar. They hear the cry of how much money can be made by ghostwriting books and the lure sends out a beacon, (remember the bat signal?) calling people into the business who are not qualified, yet, are only seeking a quick fix to their negative financial status—at your expense.

So, to help the cause, I want to outline some significant factors that need to be explored to help you recognize the "Red Flags" when talking to potential ghostwriters. As a new author, your ghostwriter search must include how to protect yourself and what to look for. Factors such as the following:

Industry Contact Influence

I spoke earlier about my mentors, my editors, and my literary agent. One marketing tactic I do not use is proclaiming my relationship with these individuals as a shady marketing tool to acquire more writing business. Finding a ghostwriter who immediately boasts on their web page, social sites, and email that they have influential industry contacts with major publishers and literary agents should be perceived as a first MAJOR red flag.

A professional ghostwriter does not need to flaunt their connections to entice you to use their services. Having industry contacts is a significant feature to have for a ghostwriter. Still, when a writer uses these tactics to lure you in, it comes across as desperate, skeptical, and non-professional. This is a major red flag.

Remember, even if the ghostwriter does have influential publishing contacts, it does not necessarily grant you access to the publishing world. And it doesn't give you the green light to publishing your book with a major publisher. Publishing a book and being offered a book contract should be derived organically and be achieved on your own merit.

The professional ghostwriter will be transparent about their qualifications and experience and stand on the merits of their accomplishment. Professional ghostwriters will not use their industry contacts to influence you to utilize their services. For you, the only critical elements necessary for the ghostwriter to possess are experience, professional-level writing skills, and a passion for helping authors write their books. The rest will fall into place.

Rookie Writer Versus Professional Writer

When I started working as a ghostwriter, I felt overwhelmed by other ghostwriters who had what seemed to be a million publishing credits; and vast experience. I felt intimidated, confused about how to start as a newbie. I didn't let it stop me from pushing my career forward.

There are good ghostwriters out there who may just be starting. Everyone must start somewhere, and if you find a ghostwriter that matches your style and what you are looking for in a writer, but lacks an extensive writing portfolio, open your mind to the possibility.

Now, please hear what I am not saying. I'm not saying choose the cheapest guy you can find or the first ghostwriter that comes along. And I am also not saying that every ghostwriter that lacks a portfolio deserves a chance. As I discussed, there are terrible, low-cost new writers out there. Yet, there are many skilled professional new writers to choose from as well. The hard part is filtering through who is good and bad. I am advising you to use your best judgment on choosing who works best for you and your book. Weigh all of the options and ask for their existing portfolio of current writing samples. Don't be shy. Ask for a specific writing sample based upon your category and evaluate the sample. You could go as far as to ask them to write a pitch package about your book as a sample to assess their writing skills.

Through your search, don't go after the next shining nugget. Be cautious with those ghostwriters who declare they have hundreds of books published and or say that have written for thousands of authors. Yes, some highly sought-after prolific ghostwriters may make these claims, but declarations such as these must be taken as a red flag.

Why?

It's simple—time and numbers. I have been ghostwriting now full time for over six years, and over the span of those years, I was able to produce and write over fourteen books. This may not sound like a significant accomplishment, but I assure you, in the world of writing and ghostwriting, it is an endeavor worthy of mention.

These books did not include my own books, and each of those books was either published with major publishers or self-published. Yet, one aspect I understand about myself is I believe I am an adept writer and can write at a moderately quick pace. Even with my skills, I could never imagine having hundreds of books written in a few years.

Also, if possible, you need to ask how long the books were and what quality they published. The reality is that ghostwriting hundreds of books would be virtually impossible to accomplish in a short time, even with a lifetime of writing. Authors like James Patterson and others churn out a ton of books, but they employ multiple ghostwriters to achieve this feat. (Yes, James Patterson uses ghostwriters.)

When I see different ghostwriters boast they have written hundreds of books, I ask— how? I know the amount of effort, hard work, and time it takes to write a marketable manuscript. On average, it takes about three-six months with an average word count of 30,000-50,000 words. So, anyone who claims they have hundreds of books would be, in my humble opinion—exaggerating a tad. Writing these many books by one person is nearly infeasible or near impossible. This is a major red flag.

Most ghostwriters are business owners who provide a service to new authors. Some ghostwriters have been published, and others have not. You will find many writers out there who claim they have multiple major publishing credits to their name. Most of the time, these are actual statements made by successful ghostwriters; however, be cautious, because some of these writers may not be so forthright.

Remember, in most situations, you will not be hiring a best-selling writer, even though I hope you do. I hope that you will be hiring a professional business writer who is transparent and honest in their business endeavors.

Recognize your goal and hire a ghostwriter who possesses the skills, along with the know-how, to write a professional manuscript that exceeds your own capabilities and expectations. Any ghostwriter who boasts significant claims of multiple large catalogs of published works— ask to examine their entire portfolio. Any pushback here would be a red flag.

Ghostwriters Who Farm Their Services Out

I was recently in a situation where I was approached by a well-known ghostwriter and was asked to help him ghostwrite a book for one of his clients. I was excited and jumped at the chance to work with this ghostwriter because he is a well-respected ghostwriter in the industry. I was humbled to have been asked to be the lead writer on his client's new book.

I jumped in with both feet, and the situation began with smooth sailing until—one day, I got the call. As it turned out, the client was not fully aware of me being the actual writer for the book. When the client found out, he was more than upset, and rightfully so, because he felt that he had hired the principal ghostwriter to write his book and not someone else, who potentially did not have the skills to secure what he wanted to capture. This put me in a precarious position. In the end, I ended up being taken off the project and faced with lost time, effort, and money.

The lesson I learned was never to farm my work out to other writers. I see what can happen, and I now believe in providing my service as a "me and only me" effort. My clients compensate me for my experience and skills to write their books and not someone else.

Let me clarify that many great companies employ incredible ghostwriters to help authors. There are excellent companies such as Kevin Anderson and Associates™, The Jenkins Group™, and Book Launchers®. Those platforms are different and act predominately as the middleman, each providing a varying degree of ghostwriting and publishing services that match up the appropriate ghostwriter with their clients.

The act of farming out your book, without prior knowledge, in my belief, is a disservice if it is not handled ethically and transparently. So, be on the lookout for any ghostwriters who farm out their ghostwriting services. The only way it could be acceptable is if the ghostwriter is forthright at the onset, letting you know and allowing you to review the other writer's credentials and portfolio to determine if it is a good fit for your project. You should be afforded the option to choose whether you want it or not.

Number one, you are the author who is going to spend good money on the best ghostwriter for your book project. The last thing you need is to have everything in place, only to find out down the road, the writer you hired is not doing the actual writing. Without your knowledge or consent, things can get ugly and head south rather quickly.

Any ghostwriter you contract with needs to do the work, and it is that simple. Be aware and ask if they have sent your book to someone in another country or have farmed the work out to another ghostwriter without discussing the scenario with you. This is the wrong way to do business and is a Major RED Flag.

The problem here is obvious. You are paying for the highly sought-after skills of the hired ghostwriter. Not a ghostwriter who you have not talked to or even met; even more important, one who has less-valued skills than you expected. This is not a good situation and one you want to avoid. Your hired ghostwriter should be the one who writes your book.

I'll reiterate to make my point clear. The only way this situation is acceptable is if the ghostwriter informs you of this situation upfront. If the ghostwriter is transparent with their intentions, and you, as the author, accept the situation, this is the only way it could be acceptable. Dragos Bratasanu, author of, *The Pursuit of Dreams: Claim Your Power, Follow Your Heart, and Fulfill Your Destiny* once wrote,

"Your persistent actions are the bridge between mind and matter, between the inner and the outer. Do what you've been called to do. Do it with grit, do it with courage, do it with boldness and faith, and do it every day for the rest of your life."

Make sure your ghostwriter is working diligently on your book, and not someone else on their behalf. Be persistent here and have the courage to ask and precisely define the ghostwriter's intention and work process. If you are presented with this situation, make sure you know every detail of the new prospective writer. Insist on having your ghostwriter put it all in writing.

However, if you speak to a ghostwriter and are presented with this farming out work approach—proceed with caution. Pay attention to the red flags. Make your intentions and expectations clear upfront and get the agreement in writing. Do not fall prey to having your work sublet out to a lesser-skilled writer. This makes for a precarious and awkward situation for everyone if not handled properly and openly.

Asking Too Much Upfront

Many ghostwriters work in different ways when it comes to getting paid for their services. These various situations are what need to be paid closer attention to. To show you what to be on the lookout for, here are some standards in ghostwriting fees you should be aware of.

Most professional ghostwriters do not work "on spec" and will not ghostwrite your book for free, without money upfront. It will be challenging to find a professional writer who will work based upon getting paid through royalties on the back end unless you are a famous entity. Most, if not all ghostwriters, require getting paid for their work and time as they write your manuscript.

A competent ghostwriting agreement involves determining the ghostwriting fees based upon the complexity, topic research, and length of your book. A standard ghostwriting contract requires an upfront payment fee upon signing of the agreement and a detailed payment plan, either monthly, installments or by chapter.

Most ghostwriters do require some money upfront. Some will take half and then the rest at the end of the project. Be aware of any ghostwriter that asks you for everything upfront without any kind of guarantee that the work will get done.

If you find and feel a ghostwriter is asking for too much without learning about your project, use discretion. Engage the ghostwriter cautiously because many pressure clients into paying before determining what is involved, or before having something in writing. Use common sense and your best judgment here. If you experience this right upfront with any ghostwriter— be aware, and my suggestion would be to move on with finding another ghostwriter. RED flag for sure.

Talking About Money Before Learning About Your Project

Through your search, if you find a ghostwriter that starts talking about money as soon as you get on the phone or interview, this is a major red flag. A professional ghostwriter will learn about you, your project, what is involved, and put together a professional proposal or a Statement of Work (SOW) based upon those facts and criteria. They will not start talking money and figures right off the bat.

If you run across a ghostwriter who insists on talking about how they are going to get paid, I advise you to steer clear and find another ghostwriter. A ghostwriter that is going to talk about money without learning about your project is probably not one of real professional value. You will save yourself time and probably a lot of grief and heartache down the line by moving on.

Asking Too Little for Services

"You get what you pay for." We have all heard it. Has it always been an accurate statement for you? For me, it has. All one must do is walk into a dollar store, and within a day or so, you will see these words come true. Cheap is cheap. And worse, cheap breaks, cracks, chips and leaves a bad taste in your mouth. Has it ever happened to you?

In the ghostwriting arena, this statement rings accurate almost every time. Every one of us wants to save money, but when it comes to ghostwriting, finding one who is cheap is NOT the best route to go. Why? First, a good ghostwriter, one with few books and experience under their belt, knows how much intense work is involved in writing a book. A ghostwriter's job is not easy, and anyone worth their salt is not willing to work this hard without charging respectively for their time. If a ghostwriter is willing to work for peanuts, they must not hold much value in their time, services, or skills with high regard. And this my friend is a major red flag because somewhere there is a serious reason why. Either the writer does not have any experience or, worse, lacks the skills to complete the project.

This brings me back to being aware of who and what you are dealing with. If you are searching for good writers on websites such as Upwork®, Guru®, Elance®, or even Fiverr® because, within those sites, there is a risk in finding a suitable writer. The old saying will, in most instances, come true. *"You WILL get what you pay for!"* If a ghostwriter is asking for pennies on the dollar to write your book, you will get writing that isn't worth pennies. So be aware.

I've lost out to clients on the onset over price and affordability; the corollary to this is many have returned with projects in shambles, vast amounts of lost money, and time. Even though saving money may look enticing in the beginning, in the end, you will have a project that will not meet your expectations nor meets any publishing standards. Let's face it, your book is your baby, and do you really want to leave your baby in the hands of someone who is a bargain-basement writer or simply doesn't have what it takes to take care of it? No, you do not.

You need to treat your book, your story, and your experience with respect and search for a higher value ghostwriter and not place all the emphasis on money and fees. A lower-value lower-fee ghostwriter, will in most cases, not be the one who can champion your manuscript to be a success. My advice— steer clear—major RED flag.

Not Having a Contract

All ghostwriters and authors should work under a contract. Remember, any book writing situation must be agreed upon by both parties and signed by both parties. This contract will define all the details agreed upon. If you run across a ghostwriter who is willing to work on a verbal agreement and does not ask to have a contract signed, this is a major red flag, and you must beware.

You do not want to enter into an agreement and have a book written without a signed contract. Things could get ugly later down the road. Not having an arrangement, in effect, places you in a vulnerable position with unsteady legs to stand on. Contracts protect you and everyone involved. Not having one could put yourself in a very precarious situation— and you may even lose money.

Without a contract, your ghostwriter could take your money and walk away; and you are left with nothing but wasted time and money down the drain. Always get an agreement signed with your ghostwriter, so you do not leave yourself open for problems. Make this your golden rule. If a ghostwriter is not offering or willing to sign a contract— steer clear. Major Red Flag!

Not Being Professional

Ghostwriting is a professional service, and just like any other professional service, a ghostwriter must be professional in all aspects. We talked earlier about employing professional etiquette when approaching a ghostwriter. The same goes for the ghostwriter, which means approaching you with etiquette, politeness, attentiveness, and being willing to listen. It must be reciprocated to you to help you every step of the way.

Professionalism involves being kind and doing everything possible to get along with you and fit within your personality parameters. The number one rule taught to me by my ghostwriting mentor was this, "The author client is always right." He also taught me, "Be polite and listen before speaking." I took his words to heart, and they have never failed me yet.

If you speak to a ghostwriter and they are not acting professionally, use a lot of slang, or appear not to take things as seriously as you expect— be aware. When talking to them, if they seem preoccupied with other things or you feel like you're being pressured or rushed, these are also major red flags. These are all signs that the potential ghostwriter is not a true professional.

The last thing you want to do, at this stage, is to leave your book in the hands of someone who is not going to treat their business as a professional. You and your book deserve professional treatment, which includes being handled with respect, met with manners, and receive a dedicated tangible work ethic from your ghostwriter to get your book successfully done.

Ghostwriter Trust Issues (Confidentiality Agreements) or Non-Disclosure Agreements (NDAs)

The ghostwriting profession involves remaining behind the scenes and upholding professional, client/author/ghostwriter confidentiality etiquette. Confidentiality with ghostwriters must be held with the highest regard. I, for one, uphold confidentiality to the utmost degree regarding all my clients. Confidentiality is my number one priority, and any professional ghostwriter should have a full confidentiality agreement set in place.

I believe that an agreement of this nature needs to be sent over as soon as possible, to get things started on the right foot with your project. If a ghostwriter is not at the very least willing to have a confidentiality agreement signed—this is a major red flag. I advise you to stay away and move on to find another ghostwriter. Anyone not willing or offers to sign a confidentiality agreement, especially in the ghostwriting professional arena, is not the ghostwriter for you—a major RED Flag.

Chapter 8/ How Ghostwriter Fees are Explained

"When I discussed the nature of value, I observed that value is nothing inherent in goods and that it is not a property of goods. But neither is value an independent thing. There is no reason why a good may not have value to one economizing individual but no value to another individual under different circumstances. The measure of value is entirely subjective in nature, and for this reason, a good can have great value to one economizing individual, little value to another, and no value at all to a third, depending upon the differences in their requirements and available amounts. What one person disdains or values lightly is appreciated by another, and what one person abandons is often picked up by another."

— *Carl Menger, Principles of Economics*

Why a Ghostwriter Gets Paid the Money, They Do

Keith Richards, one of the world's s most prolific lead guitarists, wrote a sensational book titled, *"Life."* The book was an eye-opening, behind-the-scenes look into his life as a musician in the world's greatest rock band, The Rolling Stones®. Yet, I know, and the world knows, (and understands), Keith did not sit down and write his book. A ghostwriter was behind the scenes, and they did a terrific job. The ghostwriter was unnamed and received no writing credit, which in the ghostwriting world meant he or she was paid extremely well for writing the book and remain completely uncredited and anonymous.

Then you have Tony Schwartz, ex-ghostwriter for then-presidential nominee Donald Trump, who created quite a scandal with the release of *"The Art of The Deal."* Mr. Schwartz stepped out from behind the ghostwriter curtain—with one tweet. Before the tweet, the Trump plaza was buzzing as Donald Trump began to speak in front of a large crowd during the release of the book. He started talking about his reasons, qualifications, and agendas on running for president. Trump said, "We need a leader that wrote 'The Art of the Deal." Tony Schwartz's mind began racing. *If that was so*, Schwartz thought, *I, not you, Mr. Trump, should be running for president*. The next moment changed our lives. In haste, and feeling remorseful, Schwartz tweeted: *"Many thanks to Donald Trump for suggesting I run for President, based on the fact that I wrote 'The Art of the Deal.'*

My point is even billionaires, and presidents of the United States utilize the services of ghostwriters for their skills and expertise in the writing field. The skill level and the knowledge of the process is, in part, some of the reasons why ghostwriters get paid the fees they do.

Vignette

> *Schwartz had ghostwritten Trump's 1987 breakthrough memoir. He signed a deal for the book earning a joint byline on the cover, and half of the book's five-hundred-thousand-dollar advance, and half of the royalties.*

Even Hollywood stars such as Paris Hilton® and famous rock stars such as Stephen Pearcy from Ratt® and Tommy Lee, drummer for Motley Crue®, all published books with manuscripts written by incredible ghostwriters such as Merle Ginsberg, Sam Benjamin, and Anthony Bozza. These ghostwriters received writing credit or not, yet, both were compensated higher than many ghostwriters, because of the nature of the writing for high profile people. Plus, when a ghostwriter foregoes the writing credit, (remember, Keith Richards) the fees for the behind the scenes work— are extremely higher.

Before we get into the heart of the matter, which is fees and pricing, I felt led to discuss a broader topic before narrowing in on talking ghostwriting fees. The questions on the table are:

- Why does a ghostwriter get paid the amount of money for what they do?
- Why is the fee justified?

To answer these questions, I must take you back and tell you a story. When I first started out as a rookie ghostwriter, I took any job that came my way. I was green, excited, and ready to start writing a book for someone—anyone. Soon, I signed up my first client, and I dove in headfirst.

I began wading through the trenches, word by word, meeting after meeting, transcript after transcript, and recording study. I wanted to capture the client's voice perfectly. I soon realized the countless hours I was putting in on the project. The author was an extravagant person, not challenging to work with, only hard to keep up with. The pace was grueling, and I was not in control of the situation.

The more I wrote, the more they wanted to give me. This, in most instances, is a wonderful thing, yet, I found out quickly, that the hours I was working was overshooting by miles what I was getting paid. I was almost working for FREE and still putting in 12-14-hour days, seven days a week. I knew things had to change. I vowed I would never work by placing myself in such a vulnerable position financially ever again.

Getting back to the questions—ghostwriting is damn hard work. It is not easy to sit down in front of a computer, place your mind and soul into another person's life, their unique experience, and capture the essence of those events into words. Remember, having to write those college essays or dissertations? Ghostwriting a book is all of that times a thousand. This is the reason most new authors hire a ghostwriter because they have tried sitting down and were soon faced with the immediate challenge of trying to relive their lives through the written word. Getting those words down on paper is not for the faint of heart— and honestly, not an easy task.

Due to the length of most books, most ghostwriters work on only two or three projects a year. And during this time, the ghostwriter still has to live, eat, and pay the bills. The fees are needed because if you want and expect your ghostwriter to give your book the undivided attention it deserves, the ghostwriter needs to get paid.

Ghostwriting is an acquired skill derived through sheer hard work in developing the uncanny ability to capture another human's voice, style, tone, and diction in written form. These hard-fought developed skills have intrinsic value and impact on your book. They have value because the ghostwriting profession is an extraordinary one, filled with highs and lows, ups and downs, and an immense amount of self-motivation on the ghostwriter's part.

Let's think about it for a minute. A ghostwriter sits for hours, alone, basked in your story, leaving their real lives to the side, and places your story ahead of everything in their minds. Every day spent writing, a ghostwriter becomes immersed in the life of the author, and often, it can come at a price. W. Chan Kim, the author of *Blue Ocean Strategy*, wrote, "Find the right price for an irresistible offer, which, by the way, isn't necessarily the lower price."

Lower price usually refers to a lower value, and this is the reason ghostwriters get paid what they do. It's not just about money. It's about recognizing the influential precedence a ghostwriter takes, the responsibility of writing your story, your life, your experience, and adapt it to your liking. And this is not an easy task to do, and if it were easy, everyone would be doing it.

Ghostwriting Fees and Prices

Getting to the heart of the matter is discussing fees and pricing for ghostwriting services. I speak to many potential new authors either through email or by phone, and most want to know immediately what I charge. Money is the bottom line, but, in my opinion, the discussion should never begin talking about money. In the ghostwriting book arena—it simply can't. I never talk about money without understanding more about a project and believe the adage, *"The devil is in the details."*

There are various levels of ghostwriters around the country and world, each with differentiating fees for their services. Prices and costs are specifically dependent on the details of your book, research, etc. What type of book you intend to write coincides with finding a ghostwriter that specializes in your specific subject matter. For example, business ghostwriters (like me) tend to make more money because of the complexity of the material written, along with most of the research involved.

I know that most CEOs, Fortune 500 business entities, and large and small business leaders, expect a certain level of professionalism from a writer. They are looking for someone who can deliver a crisp, professional, marketable manuscript. These leaders rely on the expertise of the ghostwriter to guide them through the process without interruption to their business lives.

Professional ghostwriters recognize that important business people lead hectic lives, and understand that professional-level service comes with professional-level compensation. The average book can run anywhere between $35,000 to over $100,000. Some ghostwriters earn over $150,000 per book. Maybe this seems astronomical, yet, as you get into the writing of the book with your ghostwriter, you will begin to understand the complexity of the process along with intricacies.

Most books take three to six months to write, and the reality is ghostwriters need to live and pay their bills while giving your book the undivided attention it deserves. So, $35,000 for the writing of your book on a professional level, while allowing you to go on with your life and business is indeed— a bargain. Professionals who understand business know the skill required to ghostwrite a sellable and marketable manuscript. They realize this will not come cheap and that these types of fees are not out of range. In 2011, according to the United States Labor and Statistics, writers and authors averaged $68,060 a year. [iii]

Through your search for a ghostwriter, you will discover ghostwriters who arrange their fees in different ways. Most ghostwriters are considered freelancers and charge fees based upon the individuality of each project. From a major publisher view, the average ghostwriting fee is approximately $22,800 per project, with some book projects ranging up to $120,000 per manuscript.[iv] These fees are derived if the ghostwriter receives a credit on the book cover or work. If the ghostwriter remains a total ghost without credit, the fees are extensively higher. The fees could range from anywhere between $45,000 to $150,000 without a writing credit. Be prepared to either give or not give the writer credit on your book. Understanding upfront can help you with your book's budget and any misunderstandings later down the line.

Ghostwriters Charging Per Hour

Some ghostwriters, instead of getting paid per project, decide to work on an hourly basis. These ghostwriters have discovered that their time has intrinsic value. A way for a new author to gain access to the highly sought-after skills could be by charging by the hour as it is the easiest and most practical solution.

Various projects, depending on the subject matter, may involve extensive research, and the ghostwriter recognizes the need to charge for the time in performing the research. And just like per project costs, different ghostwriters charge various hourly rates for writing and research. Once again, the hourly rate is commensurate to the skill of the ghostwriter and whether the ghostwriter is receiving writing credit for his work. The average ghostwriter, who is receiving writing credit, may charge anywhere from $50.00 to $100.00 per hour. And those writers who are not receiving writing credit may charge anywhere from $65.00 to $125.00 an hour.

As a new author, you must determine which way you prefer to have your book written, either giving the ghostwriter credit or not. Understand that the fee may be higher without providing credit.

The first step is to define how the ghostwriter prefers to work either with writing credit or not. The second step is to ask for a proposal based upon approximations of your book, equated down into a specific block of hours. Budget wise, it is essential to understand every intricate detail on what you are looking at as far as costs.

Ghostwriter Payment Plans

Many ghostwriters understand that most people do not have large sums of cash lying around. Most people can afford to hire a ghostwriter, yet, most need to make payments. Many professional ghostwriters offer payment plans to clients and help them with their budget. I offer payment plans to my author clients and provide extensive payment options to help each author determine their budgets to afford their books. In my writing proposals, I offer over six different payment options to ensure the book fits within the author's expected budget.

Most ghostwriters require a percentage down to get started. This percentage will vary among ghostwriters based on experience. My literary agent is a prolific ghostwriter, and he never works without having 50% down and then the remaining 50% percent at completion. This arrangement works for him and his clients, and he justifies this by giving the client's book the undivided attention it deserves until completion.

This payment scenario alleviates the worry of money on his end and the client until the book is complete. Some ghostwriters ask for 50% down and then the remaining on scheduled payments or even milestones. For example, 25%

down after five chapters, 20% down after another five chapters, and 5% paid at the end of the book.

However, beware (as I discussed earlier) if you find a ghostwriter that wants 100% upfront without doing any of the work. In no circumstance is this beneficial to you as a new author. If you run across a ghostwriter asking for such terms, steer clear and move on to find the ghostwriter.

Negotiating the Ghostwriting Fee

Once you start talking to a potential ghostwriter of your choosing, the next step is to negotiate the fee for the work. The first aspect to consider when negotiating is that a ghostwriter dedicates an immense amount of time and effort to a project. Good ghostwriters do not take on multiple projects per year, and their time working on your project must be compensated.

Many of the lower cost ghostwriters are in it for the quantity, write fast, and get you out the door. This is not what you are looking for because you are seeking quality over quantity. Yes, you may end up with a manuscript with a cheaper writer, but honestly, you must ask yourself, *has that writer captured your voice and style?* In most instances, they have not.

Most ghostwriters will not start work on your book without a fee or percentage of the price paid to start. As we discussed, most ghostwriters work in different ways when it comes to fees. And many ask or 50% upfront to start. For a new author like you, this may not be financially feasible, so my suggestion is for you to start the negotiation.

Depending on the agreed-upon fee, you could structure the payments to be paid at different milestones such as 20% down upfront and then divide the remainder of the fee into thirds. Develop an agreed-upon schedule to deliver the fees, such as a third after three chapters, a third at the halfway mark, and a third before the final delivery of the final manuscript.

Remember, you are the author, and you need to find a payment schedule that works for you and your new ghostwriter. Negotiate the best pricing fee that works for your budget and defines all payment deadlines. A ghostwriter/author collaboration fee is best supported by setting all payment expectations and research requirements in advance.

Prepare to provide all related notes and materials for your ghostwriter, which should help in narrowing in on the desired fee. Having the details of the work required will better allow the ghostwriter to determine a fair price for the work in writing your book.

Ghostwriting Projects on Spec

Please allow me to discuss the problematic issue of new authors asking and expecting a ghostwriter to write the book for free (on spec) with the hope of sharing 50/50 in the expected royalties from their book sales. This is a scenario that rarely happens, and do not be shocked if you ask a ghostwriter about this arrangement, and they answer by telling you a firm "No."

Once again, just like the rest of us, ghostwriters have to live, pay their mortgages, and put food on the table. Writing a book takes time, and as I discussed, it could take over six months or more. In this arrangement, there is an apparent risk made by the ghostwriter with no guarantee your book will sell. Unless you are a well-known individual, celebrity, politician, or CEO, you will be hard-pressed to find a ghostwriter willing to take half a year of their life to write your book without any money involved. For a ghostwriter, not being compensated for that time would be disastrous.

The inherent risk taken by a ghostwriter in this scenario is monumental. Allow me to repeat this— there isn't any guarantee your book is going to sell. Please understand this. I am not cynical; I am giving you the truth and the harsh reality. No author, publisher, or literary agent in the world truly knows how well a book will do. This is the reason some of the greatest writers of our times, keep writing and don't worry too much about sales and statistics. They only write the best books they have in their minds and creative palette and let the chips fall where they may.

However, every one of us has high hopes for significant success and millions of dollars, and it can happen. Yet for a fledgling author, the odds are astronomically against you, the first time out. Can you make a living with your book? The answer is yes if done correctly. Ultimately no business on the planet operates with such high risk— and no money.

Now, if you are a new author who has garnered interest and secured a major publishing deal (still no guarantee) but wishes to hire the services of a ghostwriter, many ghostwriters will work off of a flat-rate per-project basis. Possibly a percentage of the advance, depending on if the advance is substantial enough to warrant a share to the ghostwriter. Here, the negotiation between you and the ghostwriter is essential.

I work on a flat-fee project basis solely based upon each project's specific details. I have learned that no book project or author is the same, and there cannot be a "cookie-cutter" type of approach from my standpoint. It just doesn't work. I work with my new author's, and most of my ghostwriting projects are a flat fee project basis. I put together a book proposal (I will discuss in later chapters) and offer arrangements to work on the project-based upon specific word counts and research.

Most ghostwriters prefer to work with this type of fixed price pay model. Paying a flat fee provides stability, and security knowing you are getting your book written with a professional service. A flat fee is measurable, considering most are based upon word count and other variables. Here, the ghost is assured they will be able to dedicate their lives to your project and financially be able to live.

Every ghostwriting project must be entered into with everyone's eyes wide open. Every business and fee arrangement with a ghostwriter must be in writing for all parties to feel secure. The collaboration between you and the ghostwriter can be compared to a new marriage. You will be with that person for a longer duration, so the goal is to have everything in place, such as paperwork, trust, understanding of how the book will go.

Remember, ghostwriting is an acquired skill, deep and rich with years of learning the craft. A vastly paid, highly skilled ghostwriter is worth finding and exploring before signing on the dotted line; instead of just going with the first guy who comes along.

Chapter 9/How to Choose the Best Ghostwriter

One of the most important things to consider before collaborating with the ghostwriter is whether you connect with the writer on a personal and professional level. This is vital because, at any stage, if they do not share your vision for your book, business goals, or perhaps you simply do not get along, it's time to move on and walk away.

My ghostwriting relationship with an author is just like being married for a short period. If you do not feel comfortable about the ghostwriter for any reason, even if it's something simple like you just can't stand how they speak to you or treat you, then walk away. It doesn't matter why you say no to a ghostwriter, but just follow your gut instincts.

Listen to your inner feelings about how you perceive this ghostwriter to be. You may be asking, "What are the reasons for going this deep with a search for a ghostwriter?" I believe that every successful book originated with a ghostwriter/author collaboration with a distinct camaraderie. One of the reasons for this is because writing a book is a personal and intimate experience. You will be working one-on-one sharing discreet and confidential information with your ghostwriter. The relationship must be compatible, and you must be able to get along to a specific professional degree. Because you're passionate about your book, and it will be something that you want to share, you must be able to trust and feel confident in the relationship.

How to Properly Contact a Ghostwriter

Most people use manners and are polite in contacting a potential ghostwriter. The adage *"You get more bees with honey than salt,"* rings true in this case more than ever. If you are hopeful in garnering a professional ghostwriter, there must be rules of etiquette followed by you to make it happen.

I receive many emails contacting me about writing new books. However, it doesn't take me long to get a gauge on the author's demeanor. For me, it only takes a few sentences written in an email (yet, I still give the benefit of the doubt) to know the importance and stance of the new author. One of my ghostwriting colleagues, Jerry W., said, "I've received what seems like thousands of queries for my services, but honestly, I don't respond to most of them. Because...well...the people are rude right off the bat."

When reaching out and inquiring about a ghostwriter's services, you must employ professional etiquette and mannerisms. To capture a well-known and respected ghostwriter's attention, it is necessary to establish a professional and upstanding outlook of you as a new author. Once you approach with integrity, you will place yourself in a much better position to find the professional ghostwriter who has the experience level required for your book. Professional etiquette goes a long way, as you will continue to use it when contacting publishers, literary agents, and editors in the future.

How to Contact

During the initial contact, whether by letter or email, you should include your full name, along with a brief introduction about you and an outline, synopsis, or summary of the book. Do not write a full-length manuscript about your book. Keep your letter brief, to-the-point, and be respectful by keeping it short and concise. In the synopsis, be sure to define whether the book will be fiction or nonfiction work. This information is essential as it will aid the potential ghostwriter in understanding the project and allow them the ability to weigh in if the project is of interest.

Studying different ghostwriters, who work in your field of interest, is vastly essential as you start your search. Not all ghostwriters manage the same types of projects because some specialize, and some generalize. By including specifics about your book, and expectations of the prospective work, you can save yourself a ton of time and effort. By being direct and professional, along with providing necessary details to any potential ghostwriters, you increase your odds of garnering a high-level professional ghostwriter worthy of writing your book.

I'm human, and one of my biggest pet peeves is being belittled, and I bet I'm not alone. I receive many emails where the person is downright rude or comes out barking orders (which is never acceptable) at me before anything has ever been established. I get things sent to me, such as:

"Call me in the next hour...I want to write a book!"

"I have a book you NEED to write!" Well...are you interested?"

"I have a book...call me preferably today, but not tomorrow, I sleep in."

...And the best one I ever received to date was this one:

"I need you to call me about my book! I'm only available to talk between three and three-thirty, but I might have to cut it short because I have to pick up my kid. But call me!"

Sadly, this was an actual email I received, and I saved it for the book. I believe we can view this as an example of what NOT to say when attempting to secure a ghostwriter for your book. I didn't call any of these clients back. The reality here is perhaps these people had excellent book ideas, yet, I would never know— all from the way they approached me.

The approach you take speaks volumes as to the kind of person you are, how serious you are, and how the ghostwriter can work with you in the future. When an author contacts me, they are on the clock when it comes to professionalism and how they approach the writing of their book. I assess their demeanor, and I can now do it rather quickly.

Once again, I welcome professional new authors an opportunity to schedule a call so we can discuss their book in further detail. However, if you approach haphazardly with demands or requests that are not feasible, I will not contact them back. I know that may sound bull-headed and standoffish, but I assure you it is not. My goal is to work with excited and driven authors who know their place to a certain degree with their book. Most of the time, these new authors pan out, and books get contracted and written.

On the contrary, someone who contacts me on a whim, rude, and comes across not focused, the census (derived from past experience) leads to someone who is not that serious or dead set on writing their book. Not contacting these not-so-serious authors back saves me time and effort. Plus, in this manner, I keep my calendar open for viable projects and not time wasters.

Most ghostwriters are the same as I am. The wrong approach will get you nowhere. The hard and fast rule that stands the test of time is to be courteous, respectful, serious-minded, and, most of all, professional and polite.

Remember to remain concise and explain what direction you want to take with your book. Make sure to fill in your email subject line with a respectful phrase querying about any ghostwriter services. All these simple things go a long way in attracting high-caliber ghostwriters. Lastly, this sets the tone in starting on the right foot with your ghostwriter and the book project. Keep in mind. Respect is mutual, and it starts in the beginning.

Respect and trust need to be established at the onset. You will be spending quite a bit of time with your ghostwriter and respect and trust between both of you is necessary. Why? Because, on average, it takes three to six months to write a book, and sometimes depending on the type of subject and length of the book, it could take a more extended period. Mutual respect is essential, and you must get along. Some books have been worked on for over a year. I worked a year and a half with an author on a book just recently written for Harper Collins®. The single most aspect of that relationship was he, and I got along very well, respected one another, and understood each other. It worked because our work ethics were a spot-on match.

This is essential for you as well in choosing a ghostwriter. Not only do your personalities need to match, but your work ethics and your vision must be in line. How you get along, as far as understanding the work involved and how you collaborate to get the work done, is critical to being in sync. A professional ghostwriter will always be your personal cheerleader and a coach along the way as well. A ghostwriter should help you remain focused on the task and stay on track. They should offer helpful suggestions on how to proceed throughout the book writing process.

A ghostwriter holds many jobs and titles, but one of their primary roles is not only to write your book but to keep the project moving by eliminating all distractions and prevent you from being overwhelmed so you can complete the book project. This is important and one of the most prevailing things because many new authors find themselves in no-man's land and get lost. This leads to fear, and they never finish or get held up by the wrong distractions. I witness all the time with other ghostwriters where the authors drop off the planet and go cold. Often, self-doubt and lack of confidence creep in and delays a project by suggesting— to the author to give up. A good ghostwriter should be able to eliminate these types of distractions and avoid significant delays.

Being a professional ghostwriter takes a unique understanding of craft and ability. And not all good writers make good ghostwriters. There are thousands of great copywriters, article writers, and blog writers out there. Still, good ghostwriters are not only good at writing in another person's voice, but they also possess the skills in helping you focus and connecting with you in aspects that you didn't expect. Through your search for a ghostwriter, ensure that you partner with one that understands you and will guide you and your book to success.

As a professional ghostwriter, I've learned many techniques and what it takes to see a book come to reality. When it comes to ghostwriting your book, your goal is to choose a writer that not only possesses the necessary skills but one in whom you trust and feel good about. Once you decide on a professional who is right for your book, the chances your book will succeed does drastically increase. Additionally, you want to ensure that you endure an enjoyable book writing experience and make sure you enjoy the ghostwriter's presence and talking to them.

Throughout the book writing process, there will be many detailed and private conversations between you and your ghostwriter. Most, if not all, book projects take working together for several months, and you want to make sure that you feel comfortable with your new writer.

Do yourself a huge favor, when talking to a potential ghostwriter, outline your expectations, goals, vision, and desires, upfront right from the start. Present your research and notes. The goal is for you and the ghostwriter to have a clear understanding of your intentions for your book. Both parties should know exactly what is expected from each other; this includes deadlines, proofreading, editing, meetings, schedules, length of the book, style, and any necessary information that needs to be gathered. If you need these tasks performed with your book, be transparent and inform what is required for the proposed subject matter, such as interviews, phone calls, and in-person meetings, along with weekly checkups and updates.

One key central factor in hiring a ghostwriter is understanding your book's budget. Knowing what you're willing to spend before approaching a ghostwriter is essential. According to the writer's market, the average ghostwriting fee is $35,000 for a book. Some highly sought-after ghostwriters command prices ranging from $75,000 to $150,000 and more. Be aware there are specific situations between ghostwriters and clients where the ghostwriter agrees to a particular fee and then partakes in a share of the royalties, plus a writing credit on the book cover.

However, if you are a new author, known amongst your peers, friends, and family, but unknown to the world, these situations will not be available under most circumstances. The risk would be far too considerable for the ghostwriters to take upon themselves. These situations usually work best with people like celebrities, politicians, or even clients with massive platforms and outreach.

Be prepared to invest in your book and your ghostwriter. It will be hard to find a good quality writer under $20,000, so if you are not willing to invest in at least $20,000 for a book—stop right now. Do not pursue a ghostwriter. And yes, you can find someone cheaper, yet, you know the adage, "You get what you pay for." Do you really want to put your life's work in the hands of an amateur or novice writer who does not possess the skills necessary to write a great book? In the long run, would it be worth it? The answer would be a definite— no.

Being Transparent

Upfront at the onset, locate a ghostwriter that is transparent with you and vice versa. Be open with your writer about who you are, what you have done, been through, and even what you believe in. This is the time not to leave anything out and leave nothing to chance. The more the writer knows and understands about you, the better the book project will be. Understanding what makes you tick will help the ghostwriter provide the best writing for you.

Chapter 10/ Ghostwriting Contracts Explained

"I don't sign contracts for my books."

- Andrew Vachss

I included this quote for a specific purpose. First, I am not advocating this advice by saying, "Don't sign contracts." On the contrary, his referring to contracts shows that they are essential in the ghostwriter/author collaboration, and even Mr. Vachss has recognized and alludes to the existence of contracts (he just doesn't sign them). One of the essential aspects to understand with an agreement between you and a ghostwriter is that, in most instances, the ghostwriter gives up their rights to the ownership of the work.

The ghostwriter, by agreeing to the contract, signs over these rights to you as the author for a specified fee. Ghostwriters exchange their knowledge, their writing skills, and expertise of their craft, plus dedicate their time in exchange for monetary gain. Yet, every book is a gamble for a ghostwriter because the book could go on to sell millions (and we hope it does). The profits generated by the author in these scenarios far outweigh the compensation to the ghostwriter. These are the chances ghostwriters take and why it is imperative to have a contract in place.

Besides fees and compensation, a contract defines the role of each party within the project. To be clear, everything belongs to the author, including the copyright with a ghostwriting contract. All writing belongs to you as the author and should never be owned by a ghostwriter. Once again, to clarify, a ghostwriter agrees to fulfill a particular task by writing the book or literary work in exchange for a payment. Herein lies the risk a ghostwriter takes.

A contract between you and a ghostwriter should define the responsibilities of each party throughout the contract term. Along with responsibilities, you should have the definition of the rights of each party specified in the contract language. A ghostwriting contract should include:

- All deadline dates
- The number of revisions
- Payment terms
- Specific milestones
- Scope of the project (specifying the number of words or pages to be written)
- A definitive confidentiality agreement

Hiring a ghostwriter involves many necessary steps, and I felt that the business side should include an understanding of the contents of a ghostwriting contract as being an integral aspect before you start work. Remember, hiring a ghostwriter for your book, whether it is a business book, fiction, memoir, autobiography, the ghostwriter is considered a "work-for-hire." This entails you, as a new author, to possess specific rights necessary to protect yourself in the contract agreement; everything from copyrights, and confidentiality, which ensures your information and written work is protected in writing. (*Quick disclaimer: Please seek legal advice on all contracts if you do not understand or have questions about the contents.*)

Review your ghostwriting contract with an attorney experienced in copyright and intellectual property law before signing. The main concern is both parties agreeing to strict confidentiality and adhering to specific milestones, payments, and tasks outlined in the agreement. Writing a book involves large sums of money, and when it comes to money, an attorney can pinpoint discrepancies and potential problems with the contract. When you have a situation that includes vast amounts of money, a contract is critical because, where money is concerned, things can go wrong—in a hurry.

The ghostwriter/author collaboration is a unique business relationship that must be approached like any other business venture. None of us can predict the future and foresee any problem, challenges, or bumps in the road. Initially, no matter how well you and your ghostwriter get along, problems can arise in a work-for-hire ghostwriter/author agreement situation. To protect yourself from these kinds of issues, understanding the verbiage, contents, along with all expectations of the ghostwriting contract is essential.

The contract is the bedrock foundation guideline of the collaboration, outlining the expectations for both parties. Here are the contents of a general ghostwriting contract to allow you to familiarize yourself and help you in the acquisition of your ghostwriter. Most ghostwriting contracts should include, but not necessarily limited to:

CONTRACT NAMES: Names of all parties. Make sure to write the full legal name you wish to have in the contract.

CONTRACT PURPOSE: The purpose section outlines the specific purpose within the ghostwriter agreement. Here you will find all the pertinent details, including book description, approximate word count and pages, a tentative title, along with any other details attached to the book's agreement.

CONTRACT PROCEDURES: This section defines how you and the ghostwriter will collaborate on the project. This details how you will communicate, meet, and an approximate timeline for both parties to adhere to during the book writing process.

BOOK PROJECT PRODUCT: Here, you should have a full outline of the work expected to be completed. Be specific as to who will be doing what tasks. Describe in detail the exact work expectations, deadlines, and duties of both parties.

PLAGIARISM: This is an essential section that will enable you to protect yourself in the future of any accusations of plagiarism. The section should be explicit, declaring the contract to include all original work. Make sure whatever notes or research you provide the ghostwriter are your words and work. If you are using someone else's work, make sure they understand it is not original work. Make sure to explain your sources when you provide any materials to a ghostwriter. This way, the ghostwriter will give proper credit to the original source provider.

CONTRACT REVISIONS: This section is an integral part because it outlines how many rounds of revision are allowed for you, the author. Here, specifics should be in writing about how the revisions will be implemented and an additional cost if more changes are necessary past the agreed-upon limit.

PAYMENT SCHEDULE: This section outlines any agreed-upon payments and payment schedules. This should also include any down payments that both parties have agreed to, along with any payment duration terms. Be extremely specific, so both parties clearly understand the expectations. Money and payments seem to be one of the most significant issues if things go south.

GHOSTWRITER WRITING CREDITS: In this section, the contract will define if the ghostwriter will receive a writing credit or not. Be specific if it will be included in the book, and where, such as the cover or within the manuscript, if at all. Some new authors do not wish to have the ghostwriter credited. If this is the case, have it in writing.

COPYRIGHTS AND OWNERSHIP: Define precisely who owns the rights to the written work. Defining who owns the work is essential when it comes to copyright ownership.

CONFIDENTIALITY: Ghostwriting and author collaboration involves strict confidentiality. The nature of the relationship is built upon the trust that the ghostwriter will hold pertinent information you share in the highest of privacy and regard. Make sure this section includes that the ghostwriter does not share anything with anyone before, during, and after the writing of the book. Not only do you want ghostwriter confidentiality about writing the book, ensure this specific and essential requirement be included in the contract.

BOOK CONTRACT TERMINATION: This is an often overlooked and complacent section of the contract— yet essential. This is where it should be stated in full terms on how to end the collaboration if things go wrong. Make sure to include a detailed description of deposits and area locales in which a court hearing would prevail if the collaboration termination escalates. Make it clear by stating when the contract will end, and the method of termination. Be sure to include the duration days' and the process of notice required with any intent to terminate. The notice should be delivered in writing within a specific duration of time, such as thirty-days or fifteen-days.

More on Copyright and Ownership

In the contract, the copyright and ownership section appears to be an essential topic that has a desperate need to be understood. Many authors come to me misinformed, and I want to shed the much-needed light on the subject to help you with your ghostwriter and your book. So, one of the main questions I receive is who has the right to the written work? Is it mine (the author), or do I have to share royalties with you as a ghostwriter? The questions are simple, yet seem to elude most people. To address this sensitive and precarious issue, I want to share the exact verbiage I place into every contract. (*Disclaimer: Please use this verbiage at your own discretion. Please seek the advice of a licensed attorney before use.*)

In my contracts, I place the following, in the beginning, to solidify the stance by informing the potential author upfront my position as a ghostwriter in the relationship:

1.   I am not a co-author, meaning you will be recognized as the author of the book unless you specifically work with other co-authors. The publisher will know that I am the ghostwriter, and I will receive a byline in smaller print on the book cover, acknowledging that I participated in the book project.

2. *I will follow your lead in the major ideas and the research, if any, for the book. I will participate in the process creatively and cooperatively, brainstorming and contributing my writing skills, my ideas, and experience in the way, which is most satisfactory to our mutual benefit.*

3. *As a ghostwriter on this project, I understand that the main ideas for the project, namely the context and research you have developed, and the text outlined, are your property, and I have no interest in the project except as specified in this contract. I will not write books or articles using these ideas or research that might compete with your book for a period of TWO YEARS. Further, I will keep all pertinent details of our project and manuscript completely confidential until you direct me to release the information in writing with a signature of approval.*

There is more. Yet, I believe these three clauses solidify, in writing, my position within the contract and the beginning of the collaboration. Trust and transparency are essential in a ghostwriter/author collaboration, and I want to start the work on the right positive foothold.

Any professional ghostwriter you encounter should desire the same outcome and have you, the author, and your interests placed ahead of themselves. My goal is to protect both parties, so I also declare in writing the following:

- I do not own the writing work
- I do not require or want to pursue royalties from any pertinent sales of the book
- I am aware and agree the writing work is solely your intellectual property

A ghostwriter should maintain their stance and give up all rights to the ownership of their work in writing by signing over the rights to the client through the contract. The owner is the author and not the ghostwriter. Remember, this is your book and your story, and the copyright and writing belong to you, the client. Never compromise in this scenario.

For me, the author/client relationship collaboration is the most critical aspect of the entire book writing process. Make sure you precisely define the stance for any potential ghostwriter on this subject. When it comes down to a ghostwriting/author collaboration contract, the ghostwriter forfeits any rights to your work. A ghostwriter is merely the vessel in which your story will be told.

That may sound rather harsh— but business is business. I have seen and heard of contracts where the ghostwriter received royalties, a percentage of the advance on top of receiving the work-for-hire agreed-upon fee, and part ownership of the copywritten work. And worse, still received compensation. These contracts can be a nasty business and must be handled professionally and entered into with your eyes wide open. If not, unpleasant situations can happen quickly, leaving you frustrated, confused, and in the cold.

I have written many books, eBooks, blogs, and webpages, and in every single situation, I was paid for the work, yet the work belonged to the client. A ghostwriter should remain a ghostwriter and stay within their realm—behind the curtain. That is the best part about ghostwriting. I love being behind the scenes and writing, giving the author full credit and making them shine. That's my job, and any professional ghostwriter you seek should possess the same belief.

Allow me to point out that ghostwriting contracts are all different. Some include basic and simple terms, and then others are detailed with more complicated inclusions. Be alert and work smart. Never sign nor enter into an agreement unless you understand every word. I once was told by a well-known attorney, "A contract is only good for honest and trustworthy people." I disagreed with him, and I still disagree. Contracts should uphold all arrangements and agreements to protect both parties. It will save you time, effort, and vast amounts of money if done right.

A solid contract is the start of an advantageous collaboration. Actress /Singer Liza Minelli, once said, *"And what I liked most about any project, that when it was good, you had a bunch of people trying to accomplish something together, who were all acting together as one—that's' the most exciting time for me."*

Contracts stipulate how to work together and lay to rest any worries so both parties may act accordingly and enjoy the journey together. Working together with a ghostwriter should be harmonious, and the book experience, overall, should be fun and exhilarating. I have heard horror story after story about many collaborations gone awry, all because of ill intent and bad contracts. I have seen contracts so hardcore, unscrupulous, and one-sided (not in the author's favor), it seemed so dubious that the contract appeared to include the secret of who killed Jimmy Hoffa®.

Remember, contracts are tools, so both parties, ghostwriters, and you, the author, can work with a complete understanding of the responsibilities and roles of each party. Owning your work is vital, so protect yourself, your book, your business, and most of all your words.

Disputes

When discussing collaborations, I could not leave the topic without talking about disputes between the ghostwriter and you, the author. From your first love as a teenager, we all know, relationships can go wrong, often by many unforeseen factors. And no matter how carefully one prepares, life still happens, and you may find yourself at odds with your ghostwriter. When this happens, it can be a nasty disaster, and you need to make sure you can remove yourself from the agreement and the collaboration.

The contract should define the methods to follow and how disagreements and disputes will be handled. It's usually sufficient to include a paragraph stating that any dispute, if it cannot be solved by good-faith negotiation, may need arbitration. The contract should consist of a dispute and arbitration clause between both you and the ghostwriter. Arbitration, under the rules of the American Arbitration Association, reads as follows: (Disclaimer, please seek legal advice on this subject.)

"Any dispute arising from this Agreement shall be submitted to binding, and confidential arbitration under the rules of the American Arbitration Association in the state of [state] and county of [county], and any award issued in such arbitration may be entered and enforced as a judgment in any

court of competent jurisdiction. The prevailing party in any such arbitration shall be entitled to recover attorneys' fees and costs."

Collaborations are not the same in every state around the country. If your ghostwriter happens to be working in a different state, make sure you have a choice of states, (home-field advantage) in which any arbitration could be performed.

Once again, consult with an attorney to get advice about arbitration. Once there is a dispute, you will hope there is language giving you the option to remove yourself, such as the escape clause in your contract. Earlier in the chapter, I talked about getting out of the collaboration and including language in the agreement on how to do so, methods to follow and procedures to get out of the contract. Escape Clauses are necessary to protect you in the short and long term.

Sometimes, it is best to terminate a project when things aren't working out and cannot seem to be remedied or re-scoped. Be aware that an escape clause should include a predetermined "kill fee" paid to the ghostwriter. This means that the ghostwriter is fairly compensated for services rendered up to the point you intend to end the collaboration. And a kill fee should be honored professionally even if you are unsatisfied with the results. Make sure you understand, along with your ghostwriter, about the process if either party needs to remove themselves from the agreement.

Non-Disclosure Agreements (NDAs)

A section on contracts cannot end without discussing one of the most important things when it comes to a ghostwriting agreement, which is the *Non-Disclosure Agreement* or an NDA. This is also known as a *Confidentiality Agreement* in which the hired ghostwriter agrees to— basically keep their mouth shut about their role in the ghostwriting project. The ghostwriter should even agree to uphold complete confidentiality when it comes to pertinent and private insider information about your project. The hard and concrete rule to follow when it comes to confidentiality— anything you deem relevant to be held in confidence— should remain in confidentiality under this agreement.

An NDA is one of the most common and essential portions of a ghostwriter/author collaboration. This is especially true if the author is a publisher. I have never had an issue with any NDA, nor do I have any problems signing one. Presenting an NDA is one of my first steps in the process to start building the trust aspect of the writer/author relationship.

My advice is to read the NDA carefully. Even though most NDAs include massive amounts of legalese, I encourage you to read every word. Don't assume your potential ghostwriter will send over an error-free NDA. Remember, Most NDAs are written by legal professionals who use a basic boilerplate template that shines a light on the particulars of the ghostwriter's situation— and not yours. If there are changes needed that will fit within your personal and professional guidelines, don't be shy. Request that changes be made to suit you and your ghostwriter before signing the NDA.

The Bottom Line with Ghostwriting Contracts

Writing a book is a close-knit one-on-one creative process with a vast amount of confidential information being passed. Remember, your ghostwriting contract sets the necessary parameters to allow you to know what to expect for your money throughout the book writing process. Working with a ghostwriter is a collaborative process, yet, do not hesitate to be honest about what you need for your book. Approach your author collaboration professionally and manage the business end professionally to aid in having a positive professional relationship and experience with your ghostwriter your book deserves.

Disclaimer: Nothing in this chapter (or book) is intended to serve as legal advice; for that, you should contact a duly accredited attorney.

Chapter 11/How to Hire, Work with and Know the Process with Your New Ghostwriter

Now that you have the direction of your book, and an understanding of contracts in place, the next necessary and logical step is understanding the process of hiring a ghostwriter. This may sound easy, but being a ghostwriter, and after helping hundreds of authors find their way, I know it is not. Learning how to hire a ghostwriter for your book is a daunting task and the main reason for writing this book.

Before I became a ghostwriter, I never gave a second thought about the word, title, occupation, or about ever becoming a professional ghostwriter. To some wary new writers, the thought of working with another human being in capturing your thoughts, ideas, skillset, and words seems virtually impossible. I assure you, by the hundreds and thousands of books written by ghostwriters—it is not. Yet, it is human nature for every one of us to shy away because writing a book with another person involves opening up and sharing your dreams, thoughts, opinions, and secrets all in the belief your book will help others solve problems. These are monumental steps, and you can consider talking with a ghostwriter along with sharing the entire writing experience— an up-close and personal experience.

The nature of your ghostwriter search makes it easy to find that person, a skilled professional, who, you can trust to listen—and get it right. A professional ghostwriter you choose must be able to connect with you uniquely, plus possess the experience and skills to pull off your book professionally. The good news here, you will learn the best approach in finding the perfect ghostwriter to fit you and your project. You will be rewarded by learning how to approach the entire ghostwriter search the right way. Finding your ideal ghostwriter will entail placing you with a confident collaborator who will lead you to be one step closer to a successful book project.

Being what this book is about, I need to set your expectations on the straight and narrow. So, starting your search, one main question to ask is, *what can you expect from a ghostwriter?*

There are multiple aspects to expect a professional ghostwriter to do for you. For starters, if you are writing a nonfiction book, whether business, self-help, or a how-to, even a memoir or autobiography, you can expect, as the author, to tell your ghostwriter your stories and information. One of the first things to expect is for your ghostwriter to understand your direction and apply themselves to capture your author's voice, tone, and style.

Next, expect your ghostwriter to write your book, relying on the accurate information you provide, such as stories, research, timelines, and other pertinent information you deem necessary to be used in the book project. Be prepared to set aside time to allow your ghostwriter to conduct interviews with you as the author. In most instances, your ghostwriter will need to talk to industry experts, do more research, and fact check any additional information.

Hiring a ghostwriter to write a fiction book is more challenging. When writing fiction, different variables are in place, and the ghostwriter's role is not as defined compared to nonfiction. Fiction works may take more preparation on your part and more involvement to keep the book's story on track with your writer.

The first step in hiring your ghostwriter is understanding your expectations and how you want to deliver what your book is about. Some authors give the ghostwriter free reign and provide them with a title and topic and send them off to write the book. Then the are other authors who will give the ghost the beginning, and the end and the middle is up to the ghostwriter to conclude the book. When writing fiction, your goal is to find out how they work and choose to understand your book's main idea. You may be the author who wants to break your book down chapter by chapter before the ghostwriter writes the first draft. This is where the experience of your ghostwriter is crucial in completing your project the way you want.

Experienced ghostwriters will know how to help you flesh out your story ideas, characters, main points, plots, storylines, and organize your book, so it provides focus and positive direction. Your book needs to make sense to readers, and a skilled ghostwriter, whether writing nonfiction or fiction, can instruct by leading you to discover the best path in your book's interest. All these pertinent details are essential and must be considered when hiring the right ghostwriter. You want your ghostwriter to be the person who you can trust to accomplish the work and provide professional knowledge and know-how to make your book a success.

Inside Look into the Ghostwriting Process

When I speak to new authors, I usually receive an onslaught of questions. I'm glad I get asked questions because the more questions asked, the easier it is for me to explain the ghostwriting process—and understand the author—and the author understands me. A few leading questions I get asked are:

- How does everything work?
- What is the process?
- What will the standard process be like?

George P., an author I ghosted a book for was new, yet, he had been listening to people in chat rooms talk of the horrors of working with ghostwriters. "I heard they steal your money and disappear," he said. "Is this true?" I knew right out of the gate I had to show him the proper way and inform him correctly of the process and the benefits of using a ghost. This gave me the idea of putting together a compilation of the direct methods and processes I use to work with authors. Not all ghostwriters work this way. Every ghostwriter uses their own unique methods, so, ask your potential ghostwriter their process and use your best judgment if that process works for you.

My ghostwriting process follows these direct steps to write a book successfully. Every new author I work with follows this process, and it seems to be a good smooth process for every party. My book writing process is simple, to the point, and my intent is for every author to have a positive experience, along with ensuring the writing process remains moving in a positive direction. I am going to outline the process from the onset of when an author contacts me. Here are the 21 Steps of my Book Writing Process:

1. Businessperson (you the Author) wants a book written and decides to have a book ghostwritten.

2. The author contacts me about the book.

3. The author schedules an appointment to discuss the details and requirements of the book.

4. The author and I meet over the phone or Zoom® and learn about the book project and the author's vision.

5. The author agrees to receive a Statement of Work (SOW) with book/content proposal

6. Author and I negotiate terms of book proposal until both parties are satisfied.

7. The author is presented with a formal Statement of Work Contract (SOW).

8. The author receives an invoice on the first down payment.

9. The author approves the project outline, and the author and ghostwriter sign the contract.

10. The author pays the down payment.

11. Author and ghostwriter schedule our first book INTERVIEW.

12. Ghostwriter interviews author for OVERVIEW, OUTLINE, GOALS, and TIMELINE. Each chapter is recorded with audio and video.

13. Book writing begins. Ghostwriter (Me) writes the first chapter. Ghostwriter interviews author if needed, and performs additional research, and verifies sources.

14. The ghostwriter sends the first draft to the author. Author REVIEWS, REVISE, AND RETURNS chapter for finalization.

15. Steps 12-14 are repeated for all continuing chapters.

16. When all chapters are written, the author receives the book in WORD format. The author reviews the book. The author

makes final revision requests. The author returns the book with revision requests.

17. Ghostwriter (me) completes all revision requests.

18. Send the manuscript to the author for final approval.

19. Send the book to editors and proofreaders for formatting and final editing.

20. Send Author final marketable professional Manuscript.

21. Send the final invoice to the author before the final delivery of the final manuscript.

One key element to remember while working with your ghostwriter; things do go wrong. American novelist Robert Bloch said, *"The man who smiles when things go wrong has thought of someone to blame it on."* With ghostwriters and author collaborations, it may or may not be the ghostwriter's fault when things go south. Problems during the book writing process are preventable by following and implementing a few strategies to place the project on the right path. Do everything you can as a new author to help your ghostwriter be successful in capturing your voice. Provide the ghostwriter every piece of written material, recorded notes, audio recordings, or even videos to help them study you and your voice. As a ghostwriter, I know the more I immerse myself in my author's life and work, the easier it is for me to write and capture their voice.

Successful collaborations are built upon each party's willingness, trustworthiness, and accessibility. Make sure you clear your schedule each week to meet with your ghostwriter for a minimum of one hour. Make the most of the meetings by cutting back on idle chit-chat and use every minute to work on your book. Leave it at that. This allows the writer time to study the meeting information and start writing. This is a fine line because if you meet less frequently, the book could lose focus and direction. Once a week meeting is optimal for you and your ghostwriter to remain engaged and informed.

Remember, the first draft is usually a "Frankendraft" and is ugly and will not be the final product. So, allow your writer time to narrow in on your voice. Give them some galloping room and know it will take a few passes to get there. But, if you spot any major pending issues that you just can't let go of, speak up, and address them head-on. Your job is to intently review the writing, ensuring the ghostwriter is capturing the nuance of your stories, skills, mission, and ideas. Make sure you can imagine yourself in the words, and you are saying the words. As you read the draft, do you hear your voice? Make sure you do.

Keep in mind your ghostwriter is a human being, and just like every human, we all have flaws. So, don't set your expectations so high about the first draft. It will not be perfect. A perfect manuscript is only derived through many edits and revisions, so enjoy the journey by providing constructive input to your writer. Treat your ghostwriter with respect, and professionalism and you will end up with a much better experience rather than having ill-feelings between you both.

Your writer is there for you, so give them feedback on what you need and want to see. Let them know what they are doing right and what they are doing wrong. Yet, do it constructively. We all are human, and we all desire to be treated right. You want the best for your book, and the only way to get the best writing from your ghostwriter is to uplift, support, and show them you appreciate how and what they are doing with your book.

Kindness is contagious, and when your ghostwriter feels good about the work and collaboration, you will get the best work from them. The best advice I have for you as a new author is to be humble and check your ego at the door. Enter into every meeting, discussion, and the entire book writing process with an open mind and humbleness. Your book's success depends upon you working cooperatively without disdain with your chosen ghostwriter.

Your book deserves every chance to be a success, and the first step is knowing the process of hiring a ghostwriter. Many people out there frown upon the use of a ghostwriter and that ghostwritten books do not provide as much insight or value. These are untrue sentiments. Author Sara Sheridan once said, *"Copywriters, journalists, mainstream authors, ghostwriters, bloggers, and advertising creatives have as much right to think of themselves as good writers as academics, poets, or literary novelists."*

In believing in your book and upholding the spirit, hiring your perfect ghostwriter involves a deep understanding of the book writing process. Learning the process is vital to not only help you with clarity of how your book will be written but finding the writer who best fits your work ethic and personality.

Chapter 12/ How to Plan Your Book

"Don't classify me, read me. I'm a writer, not a genre."

— **Carlos Fuentes**

Main Reasons to Write Your Book

If you have ever watched the television show *Ghosthunters®*, you know that watching these modern-day plumbers turned paranormal ghost hunters is genuinely addictive. The spooky unexpected revelations of the show keep you on the edge of your seat. For me, (and maybe you too) seeing the tools and gadgets they use to detect the presence of ghosts is impressive.

Ghostwriter hunting is the same for you. You can be excited about the unexpected, and the hunt will reveal ghostwriters of all calibers. Keep your expectations on the ground and use your tools (cool gadgets) to find a professional ghostwriter. However, hiring your ghostwriter will not be easy. It is more than just clicking a few links and talking to a couple of writers. Your search should be in-depth and defined according to your book's subject, and the vision you have with your book. Any ghostwriter you hire must be in line with those visions and your personality.

The main reason for this book is to be the primary tool in your hunt for your ghostwriter. Before starting your search, we discussed the essential importance of understanding the main reason "WHY" you want to write a book. This should be the first step. Many new authors make the dreaded mistake of jumping headfirst into the process, without a direction, and what they end up with is a book lost at sea and never makes any money. Deciding to write a book is an essential step in your life yet must be handled professionally and not haphazardly. To see success with your book, it must be pursued the right way. Do not make the mistake of countless others by charging forward without a clue and no direction.

Most new authors have something pertinent to say and feel the ever-present pull to write a book. This is all good, and how many times have you heard your friends say, "You should write a book!" or you've said, "I'm going to write a book!" But the truth is only 20% percent of people who say they are going to write a book actually do write a book. And once the book is written, less than 1% of every new author sells more than 250 books their first year.

You can change these odds by thoroughly understanding your market and the main direction of your book. The terrible odds should show you that a solid book plan is essential as your foundation to assist you in finding the perfect ghostwriter. I have made it my mission to help you every step of the way. However, choosing to use a ghostwriter to write your book is a monumental decision. The humbling act in understanding you need help, and recognizing the need is an even more significant step forward in getting your book accomplished.

Perhaps you have tried, in the past, to sit down and write, but you couldn't seem to get the words out on paper. Possibly, you are a busy business professional who has something to say but no time to write it. Either way, hiring a professional takes guts and is brave because you have decided to put yourself and ego to the side for the sake of your book and allow someone who has the skills to write it for you. Good for you! You are on your way.

Depending on your situation, business, or skill, there is a multitude of reasons to write a book. However, to get started the right way, you must stringently plan for success. Part of that plan must be you defining EXACTLY why you want to write a book. Ask yourself important questions:

- What do you want to say?
- What do you want and hope to achieve?

- Who do you want to help?
- Are you hoping to build your business?
- Do you have a life story you want to tell?

The search for a professional ghostwriter begins with asking and answering these pertinent questions as part of your master plan. Planning your book should be treated the same as starting a new business. Every new business begins with a business plan (it should anyway). And your book should start by creating a brainstormed outline or mission statement detailing precisely why, and defining the reasons and hopeful outcomes you want to write your book.

Write out everything you foresee and desire to achieve with your book, dreams, hopes, and goals. Make no mistake; writing a book should be treated like building a business. If you were starting a new business, you would follow a business plan to move through the steps necessary to launch your new business. A book is the same. The beginning starts with extensive preparation for the initiative and focus of the book. This will help you down the road with your outreach and marketing to your targeted reader market.

Defined Target Reader

Understanding who your target reader is half the battle to shaping and defining a successful book. Knowing your target reader allows you to stay on target with your message, and not veer off the beaten path. To understand who your targeted reader is, it should be the one person whom you want to influence—the one person who desires to understand your message about what you want to say.

Whatever publishing route you venture with, whether self-publishing or traditional, this question needs to be answered. And if you decide to go the traditional publishing route, inevitably, the main questions editors and literary agents will ask you is, "Who Is your target reader?" As a professional ghostwriter, this is one of the first questions I ask every new author. Yet, most of the answers I hear are, "Everyone will love my story!" or, "My book is for everyone!" When I hear these responses, I know immediately the author hasn't defined who their primary reader will be.

Any professional ghostwriter you encounter should ask you pertinent questions, such as these, to help you along the way. Once again, if you speak to a ghostwriter and the conversations head straight for fees and payments—steer clear. A ghostwriter should take your book seriously and treat you and your book as a professional; that means helping you as a new author be successful in any way possible. A ghostwriter should ask pertinent questions to understand your intent, purpose, and goals to help you with the focus of your book. Defining your target reader is the essential first step for any book to be successful.

Chapter 13/ How a Ghostwriter and Author Collaboration Works

"Alone, we can do so little; together, we can do so much."

— **Helen Keller**

Helen Keller had it right, and even though deaf, yet independent, she recognized the vital fact that nothing worthwhile can be done alone. Writing is a solitary task, and one of the most isolated and personal things a person can do. And yes, you can toil on your book all by yourself, but you will reach a point where you will need the help of others. Along the writing journey, you will come into contact with editors, copy editors, literary agents, publicists, proofreaders, self-publishing professionals, and ghostwriters.

Perhaps you have finished the first draft of your book, but know it isn't polished and needs assistance. At this stage, the ghostwriter comes into the picture. At this phase, the ghostwriter can be the final "gasoline" to champion your book over the finish line. But, how does this correspond to finding and hiring a ghostwriter? Easy. Collaborating with a ghostwriter begins with the hiring of your ghostwriter. I want to turn the focus on what to do and how to interact once you do hire your ghostwriter.

For the sake of argument, I am going to assume you have chosen your ghostwriter and are looking forward to starting the process of working together. Vishwas Chavan, author of *Vishwasutras: Universal Principles for Living: Inspired by Real-Life Experiences*, wrote,

"I have always believed in the power of collaboration. Early on in my professional career, I realized that you can't develop all the competencies you need fast enough on your own. Furthermore, if you don't collaborate, your ideas will be limited to your own abilities. As a result, you will not be able to serve your clientele and thus can't achieve the anticipated impact."

Now that a ghostwriter is hired, the next step is for you, the author, and the ghostwriter to start the process of working together. Understand that this new relationship is a collaboration of various levels because it will take a distinct one-on-one relationship to produce a marketable, polished, finished manuscript. So, the very nature of the ghostwriting collaboration process is dependent on the determination of the individual book you intend the hired the ghostwriter to write for you.

The process begins by defining what schedule and methods are comfortable for everyone to work within. As an example, nonfiction and memoirs will, in most instances, require telephone or online meetings with your ghostwriter. If you need your ghostwriter to write a memoir, then you will need to plan on turning over any source materials, articles, notes you have that will help in the writing. The same goes for a nonfiction book. There will be interviews and meetings to discuss the pertinent material for the book.

I just recently experienced an author (name withheld for confidentiality) who gave me nothing but a single idea and then asked me to write their book. And I recently completed an entire 50,000-word book for an author who, once again, only provided me with a one-sentence thought. Yet, being a professional ghostwriter, hired to do a job, I was able to build an outline, table of contents, and wrote the book— all from intensive research, and speaking with the author— one single solitary time.

I do not recommend this type of work process; however, every author is different, and each has unique ways in which they want to work. I have accepted this fact and understand these are the aspects of being a professional ghostwriter.

If you have planned to have a novel, autobiography, or even fiction (over 80,000 to 120000 words), your collaboration process may include many factors and forms. You will probably be asked to provide your ghostwriter a general idea or in the least an outline. With a novel, it may help your ghostwriter if you provide a short synopsis of your story. If you have a partial manuscript, give it to them to help them get started.

For both fiction and nonfiction, most ghostwriters work with "milestones." The arrangement could be working chapter by chapter or delivering a specific number of chapters by a specified time and date. Often, many ghostwriter/ author collaborations decree completed work be turned in in either monthly or weekly installments. This collaboration method affords both the ghostwriter and author the ability to make revision requests, plus plan the delivery of revisions along with future chapters. For this method to work, you, as the author, must remain in full communication during the duration of the writing process to ensure the ghostwriter/author collaboration remains in a smooth, positive flow.

I have seen these collaborations go south and have experienced outside negative influence, damaging my relationship with an author. My author gave the current manuscript to a friend, who was an English major – not a teacher. And her friend went to town and just ripped apart the work (as an unskilled know-it-all critic.) The friend's uneducated opinion tainted the author's feelings of the writing, even though her friend didn't understand the first thing about manuscripts and the ebb and flow that happens.

My relationship with the author morphed into a daily defense of what I was doing and not doing, pushing the focus of the book entirely out of the picture. The collaboration steered in a negative direction as each day, I was defending every move, and it was getting frustrating on both parties. Yet, I am a professional and would never stoop to arguing with a client, so I decided to end the collaboration amicably. The sad part was the author's story, and the idea was a great one. Unfortunately, because of the know-it-all friend, I'm not sure if the author ever got her book written.

My advice is to avoid sharing your manuscript with friends, family, colleagues, and even English majors who do not understand how to write a book, before the work is complete. Doing so can be a surefire way to damage the collaboration process— irreparably.

Be honest, how do you feel when someone (your boss perhaps) peeks over your shoulder while you work? Does it make you feel uneasy or even frustrated? The same goes for your ghostwriter. Do not put your ghostwriter in the position of having to defend themselves against "constructive criticism." Yes, most critiques from friends or family are given with the best of intent, and then maybe not. Still, it is difficult, even for a professional ghostwriter, to perform and deliver the quality of work necessary when there are "untrained peering eyes" looking over their shoulders.

Collaboration with a ghostwriter must be kept with you and not third-party critiques. The book writing process must remain between the author (you) and the ghostwriter. It is imperative this collaboration must continue to be positive, to produce the quality manuscript you seek. If your working relationship goes south, most ghostwriters will, in most instances, opt-out of the contract.

Ending the Collaboration

If things start not to work out with your chosen ghostwriter, there must be an avenue in which to end the collaboration. As I mentioned, ghostwriters can decide to terminate the agreement, and you have the same options. Every single contract should include a clause for both parties to end the collaboration. There must and should be a way for you as a new author to move on and get out of the contract.

We have all signed contracts and understand that contracts define objectives and outlay business matters for every party to execute. A ghostwriting contract is the same, as it is written to ensure you and the ghostwriter achieve the results you want. Ending a collaboration should be a specific clause that outlines the procedures in doing so. Plus, ending a business relationship should remain on a positive note. Ending a collaboration professionally is healthy and essential for both parties.

An amicable separation is necessary in case there is ever a day that both parties decide to overcome the differences and work together once again. Famous singer-songwriter for *The Eagles,* Don Henley, wrote, *"Sometimes you get the best light from burning a bridge."* Even though those words have rung true in my life, yet in business, often collaborations come back around and achieve outstanding results. My advice end amicably— and never burn your bridges.

Chapter 14/ How to Execute Your Book with Your Ghostwriter

The scariest moment is always right before you start."

~Stephen King

Writing a book is a profound and uplifting moment in a new author's life. Your spirit will feel as if you're flying, by seeing, and hearing your word lift out of your mind and land onto the pages. Writing a book is the dream of millions, yet remember, statistics show that only 20% of people get around to doing it. By recognizing, you have a book you want to write, and embracing the need to hire a ghostwriter to do the work and setting the wheels into motion— is in and of itself— a monumental step. One that even most people never seem to be able to accomplish. Yet, even though you will not physically write your book, the work involved will still be a massive task placed in your life. So, get ready to sweat. Richard Simmons, America's favorite fitness trainer, once said, "No tricks, gimmicks, special pills, special potions, special equipment. All it takes is desire and will."

The Beginning

Thomas Edison once said, *"Genius is 1% inspiration and 99% perspiration."* Creativity, ingenuity, assertiveness, and a hell of a lot of work are necessary for starting the execution of your book. These factors must be endured by both parties. Starting to work with your ghostwriter can be a scary step, and at that moment, your inspiration should be encouraged. Please understand the muse; the root of the story cannot always be summoned at will— or controlled. Herein lies the inevitable "rubber hits the road" moment where the real work begins.

Ghostwriting is not an easy task and involves an immense amount of skill, patience, and knowledge of the craft. Even ghostwriters know that inspiration and the muse can be challenging to reach some days. For you, starting your book with your ghostwriter will involve a balance of being in control and letting go. You, as a new author, will be eager, ready, and willing to get going, but there are expectations to be understood.

I know how exciting this moment is. There isn't anything like seeing your ideas, thoughts, memories, stories all down on paper, but you must be ready—for let down—at least at first. My trusted ghostwriting mentor and instructor instructed me to come to terms with the first draft of any book, which he referred to as "The Frankendraft." Much like Mary Shelley's groundbreaking novel *Frankenstein*, Doctor Frankenstein started to build a creature, out of different parts, assembled and energized (with lightning bolts) to bring it to life.

To further explain, most books, as with anything creative, endure different phases. The first stage of a book's beginning writing is ugly. Even this book has gone through multiple phases: the first draft, revision, more revision, a round of humbleness by spending time "killing the little darlings," making the ugly drafts pretty once again.

Most writers are familiar with this term, and even the best writers in the world know first drafts are unpleasant unsightly messes. Many first drafts can be compared to children frolicking in the mud, and Anne Lamott, author of *Bird by Bird*, wrote about first drafts stunningly and transparently. She writes:

"Now, practically even better news than that of short assignments is the idea of shitty first drafts. All good writers write them. This is how they end up with good second drafts and terrific third drafts. People tend to look at successful writers, writers who are getting their books published and maybe even doing well financially, and think that they sit

down at their desks every morning feeling like a million dollars, feeling great about who they are and how much talent they have and what a great story they have to tell; that they take in a few deep breaths, push back their sleeves, roll their necks a few times to get all the cricks out, and dive in, typing fully formed passages as fast as a court reporter. But this is just the fantasy of the uninitiated."

So, how does this tie into working with your ghostwriter? Simple— be ready to work and humble yourself to the understanding that the first writings you receive from your ghostwriter will be, in most instances, sloppy first drafts.

The beginning of your book will start ugly, and your job, at the onset, is to understand this essential fact. Once you do, you won't be so quick to jump online and comb across the world in search of another ghostwriter as fast as you can. As a new author, you must give yourself over to the process, relax, and know that what you see at first, will not be what you see in the end. Be patient, and the book's writing process will go smoothly for you and your ghostwriter.

Understanding Drafts and Revisions

Revision and multiple drafts of a manuscript are necessary evils when writing a book. Another critical factor I learned from my ghostwriting mentor is never to share any writing— until it is ready. Even the first drafts I deliver are on an individual level, not perfect by any means, but always an amicable start in most cases. I know the first draft is the ever-present start to the entire book, and it has to be the best it can be before the author lays eyes on it.

I do my best to instruct my new authors on what to expect and explain how the book is only the beginning stages, and only starting the building process. This helps set the stage when I do deliver that first draft. I want the author to be pleased – and not panicked – with the knowledge that it is only the book's beginning phase.

Yet, no matter how hard I try, nor how many times I've done it, I always get incredibly nervous once I hit "send." I compare it to when I was a professional musician touring the country and spending five years as a headlining act, playing on the Sunset Strip in Hollywood. Over the years, as a musician, I've played thousands of shows, gigs, fairs, festivals, and opened for some of the most famous bands heard around the world. But, before every show—I was a steaming ball of unbridled nerves. It never failed.

Sending that first draft to a new author is the same. I'm a nervous mess with high anxiety, gripping me with anticipation of their reaction. I want the author to be excited throughout, and the only way to accomplish this is to deliver excellent writing—and that is my goal with every word on the page. Your ghostwriter should possess the same desires for your manuscript. My great ghostwriting friend, Mary B., said, *"No matter how hard I write, I get nervous as hell when sending the first draft of a chapter. For me, it is do or die and sets the tone of the collaboration."*

One of the most important things I know as a professional ghostwriter is another aspect I learned from my ghostwriting mentor. He always told me, *"Never share anything you've written with your clients until it is ready."* Now, before I share anything with the author, I prepare them beforehand. I let them know, *"What you're about to read is not the end result. It is only the beginning, and it's going to be ugly."*

Your goal, as a new author working with a new ghostwriter, is to be openminded, and trust your writer as you both will be working diligently together to make your manuscript shine. The first draft can also be compared to building the foundation and infrastructure of a new house. Drafts and revisions are an integral part of writing a book, and you, as a new author, will have a better outcome knowing these fundamental facts.

Stephen King, from his book Writing a Memoir of the Craft, wrote, "Kill your darlings, kill your darlings, even if it breaks your egocentric little scribbler's heart, kill your darlings." Revision is shaping, but also involves leaving the fluff on the floor. Input from both you and the ghostwriter will develop and shape the final product, and in the end, your book will hopefully look professional and saleable. Understand it will take multiple revisions and phases to arrive at the final product. Mark Twain once said, "Writing is easy. All you have to do is cross out the wrong words." Crossing out words is part of the revision process, which will mold and shape the manuscript. And we all know that you can't get a diamond without digging up coal.

Collaborating on a book is a thorough, creative process, and each chapter is another building link or starting point (remember Frankenstein) in reaching the final book masterpiece. I just recently finished a memoir for a new author, and she and I worked stringently on revising her manuscript. Even though the work was challenging and time-consuming, at the end of the day, she said to me, *"It is a masterpiece!"*

The ghostwriter should outline the process with you. Take their process and ask how you can make it work with your schedule for the best results. When I work with an author, the process begins with consecutive interviews for each chapter. Working chapter by chapter allows me and the author to develop rapport and a writing rhythm. And with every chapter, I express to the author that this is THEIR time. With me, as their ghostwriter, it is a "no judgment" environment, and they can speak freely and candidly. I want them to give me anything and everything. I want them to feel free, open themselves to have a conversation, and tell me their ideas, knowledge, memories, thoughts, and fears.

Once I have it all, I take those nuggets of information and mold and shape them through revisions. The plural use of the word "revisions" tells you there is more than one revision necessary to make a saleable manuscript. Revision, by standard definition, means *"to make a change, or to alteration."* And your book depends on these revisions or "alterations" to make it great.

As a new author, this is where you come even closer to the grand scheme of things. Your most essential job during the initial writing and revision stages is to be engaged and patient with your writing project. Be prepared to work, and chisel away at the drafts of each chapter as you receive them.

Be ready to remove the unnecessary and keep your book's focus within your sites. Work with your ghostwriter and ask questions. Allow the ghostwriter the transparency to provide valuable and insightful feedback to guide you through the process. Step up and provide positive communication and put your entire being into the book writing process. This is the difference in seeing success or failing with your book.

Trusting your Ghostwriter

Every relationship, whether with your parents, siblings, girlfriends, boyfriends, and spouses are reliant on the word trust. Your involvement and collaboration with your ghostwriter are built upon the same premise. When seeing the first draft or other consecutive drafts, it is human nature to run for the hills when you think something is wrong or not right. That is your "fight or flight" reptile brain working and is a normal and instinctive reaction. Your book is important to you, and in most instances, your personal reputation and business reputation will be in jeopardy if not executed the best it can be.

Seeing the unpolished portion of a first-draft manuscript can be shocking if you are not prepared. Yet, trusting your ghostwriter is crucial throughout the process. A professional ghostwriter wants nothing less than perfection, but most understand the work involved in getting there. Writing a book is not easy, and working with a ghostwriter is something that requires your undivided attention— and trust.

You and your ghostwriter must work in tandem as trusted partners, even if things seem as if they will never work out. Trust in the fact that it will. Believe in yourself, your ghostwriter, and trust in the process. A professional ghostwriter will take the reins and get you there. Being confident in the ghostwriter's ability to draft a marketable and saleable manuscript is essential throughout the process. There will be obstacles and challenges, deadlines, and time crunches, even illnesses that can delay the book, so you must trust the writer. Yet, everyone knows that trust isn't easily earned. Warren Buffet once said, *"It takes 20 years to build a reputation and five minutes to ruin it."* And I believe Peter Drucker, author of *Managing for the Future*, said it best:

"The leaders who work most effectively, it seems to me, never say 'I.' And that's not because they have trained themselves not to say 'I.' They don't think 'I.' They think 'we'; they think 'team.' They understand their job to be to make the team function. They accept responsibility and don't sidestep it, but 'we' gets the credit... This is what creates trust, what enables you to get the task done."

Trust is earned and a one-way deposit. Once trust is removed from the deposit, it can never be returned. The ghostwriting/author collaboration isn't any different. To build trust, there has to be a give and take, along with a full understanding that the process has meaning and purpose. The manuscript will evolve; it will take perseverance, tenacity, heart, willpower, and vast amounts of trust within each other to get it there. All this refers back to choosing wisely and vetting your ghostwriter for your project.

A successful book collaboration demands the ability to qualify your ghostwriter. Verifying their professional expertise and credibility to manage a book project successfully is vital. I want to make sure you are confident in your choice so you can concentrate on the book's big picture. You do not want to get into an arrangement only to discover you are spending far more time feeling anxious about what is happening with your ghostwriter—than writing the book. My goal is to ensure, to the best of my ability, that hopefully, you do not endure such a nightmare.

Communication and Commencement

Communication is essential when starting your book with your chosen writer. How you will meet and what you will discuss during those meetings is vital to have defined, so there isn't wasted time. I talked about taking this time while working with a ghostwriter to be open, transparent, and enjoy the entire process. The essential aspect of the ghostwriter/author collaboration is trust, reliability, responsibility, and massive amounts of communication.

The book process starts by gearing up and brainstorming on everything that you can think of that you want to include in your book. Brainstorming includes communicating your thoughts and revealing what is inside of you. Show the real you, and that my friend is where the great books lie. Prolific writer, Ray Bradbury wrote in his book, *Zen in the Art of Writing:*

"You must stay drunk on writing, so reality cannot destroy you. For Writing allows just the proper recipes of truth, life, reality as you are able to eat, drink, and digest without hyperventilating and flopping like a dead fish in your bed."

Communication with your ghostwriter is an essential aspect of writing to keep reality from destroying you. Another part of collaboration is the communication factor. It involves being accessible for meetings, answering emails, phone calls, or messages promptly. Open communication also includes giving your ghostwriter any notes, articles research, and everything involved to start the book. The premise is simple— avoiding open contact with your ghostwriter could delay or even derail the entire project.

Outlining and Table of Contents

I think it would be difficult to find a book that doesn't include a table of contents. Yet, in most books, that table of contents began as an outline and evolved into the final product. Once the collaboration between you and your ghostwriter has started, boundaries set, meetings, and deadlines communicated, the next phase would be to begin work on the foundational outline of the book. Some authors approach me already having a framework in mind as a starting point. Then others enter into the process organically and rely on the ghostwriter to help them define the outline and table of contents.

It does help your potential ghostwriter if you have a preliminary outline that can evolve into an official table of contents. This table of contents will be your form of guideline for your meetings and your schedules. Following the table of contents keeps you on track with chapter and other aspects of your book. It is always a benefit to be on the same page and understand the specific topics you will be discussing to keep things on track.

I use the table of contents to set up the meetings with my authors. This way, the session remains productive because each party knows what will be discussed. This system ensures that time is not wasted. We jump right into the subject matter whether we're talking about chapter one, introductions, or preface, we stick to that topic until complete.

Other ghostwriters may work in similar manners; some don't. Yet, I have found this method to be the best for my clients and me to keep the book moving forward positively—and saving time and money to you as the author.

Manuscript Editing Explained

I talk and meet with many new authors, and one of the main questions I receive is about the editing of the manuscript and how I, as a ghostwriter, address this issue. In your search for a ghostwriter, remember, editing, and the editing process is a pertinent issue you must be prepared to ask about.

Most professional ghostwriters employ different editors, but do not assume they do—you must ask. Myself for my ghostwriting business, I employ two fantastic editors to work on the manuscript after my eyes cannot see any more imperfections. I know, as we discussed, I cannot work alone, and a book takes the help of others. I send it over to fresh eyes, for copyediting, line editing, grammatical error editing, final proofing, and formatting. I started using these freelancers because I saw the need to have these editors at my disposal to ensure my author's manuscript is prepared professionally for the book market.

I personally wanted to take my ghostwriting services the extra mile and provide an incredible service. Not all ghostwriters offer these services as part of their writing package. I do, and I do not charge extra for these services. I believe it is an essential part of the book writing process and should be included in my book writing package.

Editing is a crucial factor, and as a new author, it must be something you must discuss with your ghostwriter. Ask about their editing process and procedures, and determine if it is an extra charge to you or if it is included in the agreed-upon fee.

Once edited, you should have the opportunity for any additional revisions and refinements that your book requires. All this refers back to seeing the ugly Frankendraft. When you receive your first draft, and you see typographical errors or grammatical mistakes— don't panic. Remember, the manuscript will go through stages, and along the way, it will be shaped, molded, and polished.

Yet, it will not be polished until the editing and formatting process has been completed. Trying to keep up with every minute detail and typo would be like shoveling snow in a blizzard. During the editing and revision phase, your goal is to trust your ghostwriter to make sure these things will be taken care of before your book goes live.

As I discussed, many ghostwriters utilize freelance editors and copy editors. These specialized editors work with you and the ghostwriter to ensure that manuscripts are polished and ready to go. If your ghostwriter does not provide editing services, there are also editors and people that do this type of work on websites such as Fiverr® or Upwork® that will edit manuscripts professionally. There work is steered toward making your manuscript clean, presentable, marketable, and ready to go. These are all options you must think about before your book is published.

Ghostwriter Accessibility

As part of your agreement, how and when you can access your ghostwriter should be defined in your agreement. The meeting details and how you will meet should be agreed upon and adhered to, out of respect for each other. Everyone has their personal lives, and your ghostwriter should be afforded uninterrupted personal time.

I had an author, who, even though I enjoyed writing his book, insisted on calling and emailing me at all hours of the day and night. At first, it wasn't a huge deal, but then it got worse. I did my best to set the initial boundaries, yet the author did not respect my wishes. The relationship started to become strained. Even though I maintained professionalism throughout, my privacy was being invaded slowly and surely, and it interfered with my family and personal time. Once we were done with the book, I vowed to make sure boundaries and expectations were set and met.

You and your ghostwriter should maintain boundaries and show up on time for meetings and do what you say. Be respectful of their time and yours. This keeps the relationship on a positive note and the manuscript moving forward, avoiding any glitches or hang-ups.

Chapter 15/ A Book Is Born

"I still encourage anyone who feels at all compelled to write to do so. I just try to warn people who hope to get published that publication is not all it is cracked up to be. But writing is. Writing has so much to give, so much to teach, so many surprises. That thing you had to force yourself to do---the actual act of writing---turns out to be the best part. It's like discovering that while you thought you needed the tea ceremony for the caffeine, what you really needed was the tea ceremony. The act of writing turns out to be its own reward."

— Anne Lamott

Here you are with a new book ready to be born. You now have a manuscript you are proud of. Working with your ghostwriter was a success, and you are prepared to move onto the next step. This is a significant step; it behooves you to have a strategic plan once your manuscript is complete. Yet, you are a bundle of nerves because you know that this next step is the biggest of them all—how to publish your book and what to do once you do. Getting your book ghostwritten was a major endeavor, but there are two primary questions you need to answer before moving forward:

- Are you going to self-publish?
- Are you going to traditional publish or go mainstream?

I suggest going the solo publishing route to the majority of my authors because it is a great way to get your feet wet and into the book business. It may open up doors for later offerings, potentially signing with a major publisher. Once you've shown that you can sell books and garner success on your own, acquiring a major publisher will be a little easier.

However, questions most new authors present to me are vital that I felt I needed to talk about here in the book. Your search for a publisher should start by asking yourself important questions such as should I go with a traditional publisher or self-published?

My answer to this question is never an easy one. And here is why. Choosing your publishing route, whether traditional or self-publishing, is more complicated than just a simple one-two decision. There are specific benefits and variables you must consider because the direction you choose will have a major bearing on your choice of ghostwriters you are seeking— and here is how and why.

There is a multitude of ghostwriters out there who specialize in different subjects and categories. There are those ghostwriters who only write for business or focus on only fiction. Then there those ghostwriters who focus their craft on only nonfiction books, memoirs, how-to, or self-help. To narrow in the right choice with your ghostwriter, you must decide first, which publishing path you choose—self-publish or traditional publishing.

If you are planning to self-publish, then your ghostwriter search begins with locating the person who specializes in your category of interest but also possesses the skills to help with the process of self-publishing your book. Some ghostwriters charge extra fees to coach you through the self-publishing process, and if you have never self-published, this is an excellent aspect to have can consider.

I personally coach my new authors as part of my service. Yes, I know it is an extra step, but I'm here to help anyone with their dreams. Plus, the way I see it, every author I help is another book born into the world and, in my opinion — is an excellent thing.

If a ghostwriter does charge a fee for book coaching, it may be worthwhile to endure the cost to learn the rigors of the self-publishing process. Once you learn the ropes, it will be easier for your next book. When self-publishing, it is a straight forward choice for you to evaluate different ghostwriters and their past work in your field. Choose the ghostwriter who you feel most confident in who can deliver the style you envision.

Self-Publishing

Self-publishing has grown by massive proportions over the last few years. The opportunities to self-publish your book across the internet and the world is at your fingertips, and more advantageous than ever before.

If you're considering your option to self-publish your book, you're not alone. Studies have shown that the Big-Five traditional publishers now account for only 16% of the e-books on Amazon's bestseller lists. And self-published books now represent 31% of e-book sales on Amazon's Kindle Store®.

The best news is that self-published book authors are now earning nearly 40% of every e-book dollar. Gone are the days where books are frowned upon because they are self-published. Self-publishing is a viable and respectable path to take with your book, and according to other studies, self-published authors are leading the race. They have been reported to now be taking "significant market share in all genres."

One of the essential benefits of choosing self-publishing is that a new author has complete creative control. Unlike traditional publishers, where you, as an author, are subjected to the direction of publishing teams, editors, and creative directors, you have full control of your self-published book.

Self-publishing involves four distinct phases that must be completed to reach the final product. These stages include the writing of the book – hiring a ghostwriter phase, revising, and editing, designing the cover, and lastly, publishing and printing. And within each stage, there is the need to choose and hire professionals to handle the workload necessary to make your book complete.

The first stage is hiring a ghostwriter that fits your style, voice, and direction for your book. Remember, excellent writing is critical to your book's success. All the fancy cover design and marketing of a horribly written book— can't save it or make it sell. It won't happen. The writing of your book, if you do not possess the skills, must be handled professionally by a skilled tactician of the written word.

This is where choosing a great ghostwriter is essential at the onset of your book. Do your due diligence and choose wisely because hiring a cheap ghostwriter who writes a bad book— is a waste of time. Your book will never get off the ground.

A benefit of self-publishing is that it allows you to work for yourself and create your own book empire. Author Joanna Penn, in her book, Business for Authors wrote:

"I was a business consultant for 13 years before I gave up my job in September 2011 to become a full-time author-entrepreneur. I worked for large corporates and small businesses, implementing financial systems across Europe and Asia Pacific.

I've also started a number of my own businesses, a scuba dive charter boat in New Zealand, a customized travel website, a property investment portfolio in Australia as well as my freelance consultancy. I've failed a lot and learned many lessons in my entrepreneurial life, and I share them all in this book.

In the last six years of being an author, through tempestuous changes in the publishing world, I've learned the business side of being a writer, and I now earn a good living as an author-entrepreneur. I'm an author because it's my passion and my joy but also because it's a viable business in this age of global and digital opportunity." [v]

Working for yourself affords you the freedom to not have to answer to anyone else as every choice is yours—good or bad. And self-publishing can be done cost-effectively. Now, notice, I didn't say FREE or cheap. I said cost-effectively, which would indicate that there is a cost involved. We all know that there is not anything FREE in this life.

I want you to remove these thoughts right now from your head; you cannot do a book without outlaying some money. Self-publishing, done correctly, does take money to get your book published, and hiring a ghostwriter could be and should be considered part of those costs. Think of writing a book like starting a new business; you are creating your own inventory. Upfront, you will need money for a ghostwriter – a good one – to write the book; and next, book design, then advertising and marketing.

The key is to plan your book as if you plan any business. Create a master book plan and prepare your budget for these costs. However, some of these costs can be reduced if you're savvy, thrifty, and make the right decisions. However, I reiterate, do NOT go the cheapest route with everything, especially the ghostwriter. The old saying goes, *"If you spend cheap, you get cheap,"* and this holds true in the self-publishing world.

Yes, you may save dollars on design or marketing, but please (I beg you) don't go cheap with the writing. Hire an excellent professional ghostwriter to generate a marketable and saleable manuscript. Give your book a fighting chance, and don't allow yourself to be lured into saving money with a cheap writer.

I had a client, Traci J., contact me about her book. Our conversation went great, and I thought we would work together. Yet, a few days later, she contacted me and said, *"I found a writer who will write 80,000 words for $500.00. I like you, Jeff, but I need to go cheaper for my budget."* I did not attempt to convince her to make another decision and go with me. Why? Because I knew I would not have to. A few months later, Tracie emailed, *"Jeff, I made the wrong decision. The manuscript is a complete disaster, and all I got was wasted time. When can we meet to have you write my book?"*

Spending your money where it counts by hiring a solid professional ghostwriter is the safest route to take. A well-written book will sell, find an audience, and allow you to reap significant financial rewards. With self-publishing, since you incurred the cost of your book, you will enjoy earning back every dollar of every book you sell because there isn't any middleman and most, yet not all, come straight to you.

One route I see most new self-published authors take is advocating a portion of their proceeds for further marketing and advertising of the book to generate even more sales. Once you begin to generate a profit with your book, many new authors start saving for their next book—and repeat the process.

Having multiple books strengthens your brand and portfolio while getting your name out there among the masses. Writing a book on your own is a self-gratifying effort. It will take patience, perseverance, and drive. Once accomplished, you can hold your head high, knowing you were able to make your dreams true.

Traditional Publishing

Mainstream publishing is still a notable achievement, yet, the significant irony to it all is that the major perks that come with traditional publishing such as marketing, editing, book design, etc. are now on the same level playing field as self-publishing. New authors, no matter if going mainstream or solo, have to plan on performing all of these factors in championing the book to success.

I had one of my authors I had written for in the past approach me about writing a new book for him. He informed me he had decided not to self-publish, and he wanted to pursue a traditional publisher. Having secured a few books deals myself over the years, I know how hard it is to pursue a major publishing house. My author was amazed and, at first, doubted what I was telling him was true. *"I thought getting a major publisher would be easy since I have many other books,"* he said.

Most of the time, he would be right; having a stable of books in your arsenal, and a thriving platform of dedicated followers does help in acquiring a publisher. But, having many books does not guarantee you a seat at the table. It helps but is not a promise. This brings me back to choosing the right ghostwriter, who understands what it takes to gain a major publishing house.

Traditional publishing is what every author aspires to achieve when thinking of writing a book. However, just like my author friend, I have found that most new authors believe it is easy to gain a traditional publisher. It is not.

Many fledgling authors think it is just like flicking on a "switch." Be assured I am not raining on your parade, and I am not throwing negativity around. But in being forthcoming, it is majorly challenging to get a traditional publisher. Acquiring a major publisher involves an immense amount of work, plus a thorough knowledge of the topic you are writing about.

Traditional publishers want new authors to have an established audience or platform. Having multiple books helps build your platform, and alleviates the risk traditional publishers take when publishing a new book.

Literary Agents and Book Proposals and Ghostwriters

Pursuing traditional publishers involves acquiring the attraction and attention of a literary agent. In doing so, it brings me back to searching for your ghostwriter. To gain a major publisher, you will need to seek representation from a literary agent. There is the necessity to write a book proposal and book pitch to increase attraction and interest in you and your book. Having a well-written book proposal is critical to have to pitch your book idea to major publishers. A skilled ghostwriter can be employed to write a selling book proposal to garner the attention of agents and publishers. I recently spoke with my agent on this topic, and he told me:

"Gone are the days when agents could pick up the phone and drum up interest about a new author. Publishing houses need to have something to sell and must present book ideas to boards, committees, and editorial decision-makers. A solid, well-written book proposal is not a luxury—it is a necessity in today's publishing world."

A book proposal consists of many specific variables, including sample chapters and introductions about your book. To attract the attention of literary agents, having this proposal is a must.

I have written multiple book proposals that ended with successfully selling each manuscript, two of which ended with Big-Five publishers. My understanding of the book proposal writing process is secure, but I understand that there is always room for improvement because a book proposal writing takes immense skill. A professional ghostwriter should be able to write a winning book proposal, but keep in mind some may not have the skills. You must ask upfront if you need a book proposal written and put it in writing as part of the contract. So, yes, perform your due diligence and ask beforehand.

Having your ghostwriter write the proposal along with the first two sample chapters allows you to get to know your ghostwriter, their writing skills, and how they work. I have spoken with other notable ghostwriters, and some suggest writing only the book proposal first, before writing the entire book. This way, you can pitch your book and idea to literary agents and publishers to generate initial interest.

If you sell the book, then you will have a duration of time, specified in the contract, to write the rest of your book. Remember, there aren't any guarantees in your bookselling. Writing an entire manuscript for a publication that won't sell can be a gamble, and this book proposal approach is something viable to consider. Plus, as you work through the first few chapters, it allows you to define the direction of your book. Having a defined direction with your book increases the odds of gaining an agent and a publisher.

Traditional publishing is prestigious and carries a meaningful message across the industry that you are a professional author. Yet, before you decide to choose this route, you must understand there will be an immense amount of work to get there.

We discussed earlier that self-publishing, even though easy to do and if you do it correctly, will take different amounts of money to get in the game. Traditional publishing provides you the luxury of not spending your hard-earned cash, as they publish and design your book with their in-house design teams. Plus, the publisher introduces your book to their network of bookstores and book buyers across the nation and the world. You, being a traditionally published author, now do not have to worry about these essential steps.

However, most traditional publishing houses do not have enormous marketing budgets, afforded many authors in the past. As a new author, even with major publishing, expect to use your own money for speaking engagements, book signings, and marketing of your book alongside the major houses' own marketing efforts.

Traditional publishers, if interested in your book, will offer an advance toward royalties on your book. This advance is money to help you live while writing your book.

These advance fees can be used to hire your ghostwriter for the project, plus help you save time by getting your book written quicker.

Getting a major publisher comes with perks and prestige. Yet, the tradeoff is you do not have all the control, and you must pay back the advance before royalties are fully dispersed to you. In turn, you get to enjoy the immense marketing and wide-scale distribution most major publishers have in place, saving you time and effort in acquiring these channels.

One significant advantage is once you get a major deal, if done right, you can look forward to other future book deals. Being in the big leagues is something to be proud of. If it is your dream to have a book published with a major publisher, you must perform the right steps to achieve your dreams. The first crucial step in all of these endeavors— acquire a sound, skilled professional ghostwriter.

Chapter 16/ Ghostwriter Hunt Finale

"It is in the doing that makes the being worthwhile."

~ Jeffrey Fry

As a professional ghostwriter and author, I know through trial by fire that writing books is not an easy task. Choosing to hire a ghostwriter is not an easy task either. I recognized this factor as being a monumental endeavor for many new authors— and is the sole reason for this book. My goal is to earnestly help you along your new book journey and find a ghostwriter best suited for your book.

No matter how you roll the dice, whether you are a business leader, CEO, President, celebrity, small business owner, it is incredibly challenging to write a book and see your book come to fruition. Yet, we all know that anything worth pursuing is worth doing it right. Plus, every business owner/entrepreneur knows that it takes a good hard push to get a ship to sail. But once your ship is sailing, most of the time, it will sail smoothly across the waters.

However, you and your book, just like a ship, will meet rough seas and storms. Those storms arise from the efforts of your book marketing and book process, but in the end, if you keep pushing and you keep driving—your ship will eventually arrive safely into the horizon. Hard effort must be put forth or your book to do well and see success.

Being a business owner on multiple occasions throughout my life, I believe in business and entrepreneurship. I also believe in new authors, like you, seeing your book dreams come to life. I love books and, over the years, have immersed myself within the confines of the greats: Stephen King, James Patterson, Malcolm Gladwell, to name a few. I know that this same passion for books, and the drive to help new authors create new works, is what made this book possible; although I hear all the time that the world doesn't need another book and that the industry is saturated with millions of books. And yes, this is true.

Remember, those million books are not my book, and those million books are not your book. Only you can write a unique book and bring to the world your one-of-a-kind story. You are the only you, and it is your life light, filled to the brim with memories, experiences that make up the center of your life. No one has experienced or lived your life— only you. What you bring to the table through the written word is something no one else in the world possesses. That is something worthy— and exceptional. No one else has lived your life for you, and this is the magical factor in writing your book. The book within you can only be written by you.

I have loved ghostwriting books for authors around the world, and my goal with each book was to help that author help others achieve their success in their entrepreneurial pursuits. My ultimate goal with this book is to help you because I love to help people, and I love to see businesses, entrepreneurs, and individuals flourish. And it inspires me to see people pursue their dreams, following through the process— one step at a time—and make their dreams a reality.

But the one thing I know, more than anything else in the world— if you dream of writing a book, let nothing stop you from making happen. Having a book is an essential and critical step to having a successful business—and a fulfilling life. Not everyone, as we discussed, writes a book. Very few do. However, whatever your business may be, whatever you have experienced or whatever your goals are, a book is a direct way to put it all into words. A book is a straightforward method of individualistic expression.

The value and thrill of writing a book depicting your skills, know-how, and life experience— is unmatched. A book transcends your expertise and delivers your words that will hopefully live on to help millions of others for many years to come. So, go, write, open your mind, and in the words of Ray Bradbury, in *The Zen of Writing:*

"Run fast, stand still. This is the lessons from lizards." What can we learn from the Lizards, lift from birds? In quickness is truth. The faster you blurt, the more swiftly you write, the more honest let your muse run like a gazelle." [vi]

I believe you can achieve every dream by exposing your life to the written page. Choose wisely your ghostwriter and enjoy writing the words that lie deep within your heart. Hire your ghostwriter, be inspired, trust, and deliver to the world a book—your book— the book that only you can write. Gail Devers, the two-time Olympic Champion in the one-hundred meters for the U.S., once said:

"Keep your dreams alive. Understand to achieve anything requires faith and belief in yourself, vision, hard work, determination, and dedication. Remember, all things are possible for those who believe." [vii]

Push for your dreams of having a book present in the world. Above all— believe in yourself. A book, with all of its magic contained, is an achievement; once done, no one can take from you. Choose the perfect ghostwriter to be by your side, your guide, and your confidant through your journey. Achieve greatness— I believe you can do it.

About the Author

Jeffrey Mangus has ghostwritten business books for many independent business authors and some BIG-FIVE Publishers, including HARPER COLLINS, HARPER COLLINS LEADERSHIP, ROWMAN & LITTLEFIELD, and HIGHBRIDGE AUDIO. He is the author of his new upcoming book AMPOSSIBLE (2021) for Rowman & Littlefield and represented by Literary Agent/ Gary M. Krebs of GMK Writing and Literary Services.

Jeffrey brings over 25 years of experience as a business writer, ghostwriter, and blogger, with many published books and eBooks. Jeffrey delivers to every new author real-world experience, expertise, dedication, and extreme professionalism to every word on every page on every book assignment.

Jeffrey specializes in ghostwriting for business leaders, business owners, entrepreneurs, celebrities, musicians, politicians, CEOs, literary agents, major publishers, and corporate entities with ideas and dreams of having a book or multiple books dedicated to their specialties and skills.

On a personal note, Jeffrey was a professional touring musician. He has recorded four albums and was signed to two independent record labels. Jeffrey and his band STEEL ROSE headlined the sunset strip (1988-1992) playing historical venues such as the Whisky-a-Go-Go™, The Roxy Theatre™, and world-famous Gazzari's™. He toured the country and opened for major rock groups and headlining acts such as: Molly Hatchett®, Black Oak Arkansas®, Little Feat®, Jackyll®. And Jeffrey opened for many famous blues artists, Bryan Lee, Jason Ricci, and The New Blood and Chicago Blues Artist of the Year Nick Moss.

Jeffrey worked in the healthcare field in cardiovascular surgery as a perfusion technician for twelve years. He is a retired broker/owner of two multi-million-dollar real estate companies and enjoyed a 14-year real estate career before turning to a full-time ghostwriting career.

If you would like to learn more about Jeffrey A. Mangus and his ghostwriting services, Schedule a FREE no obligation book consultation. Please visit http://www.ghostwritingusa.com or contact him by writing ghostwriterusa1@gmail.com

Sources

i https://www.theguardian.com/small-business-network/2013/mar/13/james-caan-market-research-startups

ii https://blog.hootsuite.com/linkedin-statistics-business/

iii http://www.dl.gov

iv http://www.dol.gov

v https://www.amazon.com/Business-Authors-Author-Entrepreneur-Writers-ebook/dp/B00MQTR9HA

vi https://www.goodreads.com/book/show/103761.Zen_in_the_Art_of_Writing

vii https://www.azquotes.com/quotes/topics/believe-in-yourself.html

www.ingramcontent.com/pod-product-compliance
Lightning Source LLC
Chambersburg PA
CBHW071357210526
45465CB00001B/126